# BE A STAR!

## Francess Lantz

Troll

Copyright © 1996 by Francess Lantz.

Published by Rainbow Bridge, an imprint and trademark of Troll Communications L.L.C.

All photographs by John Landsberg, except for pages 10, 18, 25, 40, 52, 74, 87, 91, 109, 142, 161.

Excerpts from *Kids on Camera: A Comprehensive Guide to Child Modeling and Acting* © 1990 by Eva Stancil. Used by permission of Peachtree Publishers, Ltd.

Excerpts from *The Young Performer's Guide* © 1990 by RECAP Publications, Inc. Used by permission of the authors.

Cover design by Tony Greco & Associates.

Printed in the United States of America.

10  9  8  7  6  5  4  3  2  1

For my mother,
who always makes me feel like a star

# TABLE OF CONTENTS

1. RICH, FAMOUS, AND UNDER EIGHTEEN　　9

UP CLOSE AND PERSONAL:
SHAWN TOOVEY　　24

2. STARTING SMALL　　32

3. MOM, CAN I BE A SUPERSTAR?　　44

UP CLOSE AND PERSONAL:
CYNTHIA AND JIM TOOVEY　　58

4. SMALL-TOWN HEARTTHROBS　　64

5. WHEN AN AGENT IS THE ANSWER　　75

UP CLOSE AND PERSONAL:
OLIVIA HACK　　90

6. STRUTTING YOUR STUFF　　96

UP CLOSE AND PERSONAL:
PAUL SUTERA　　108

7. I GOT THE PART!　　114

8. MAKING YOUR MOVE TO THE BIG TIME　　130

UP CLOSE AND PERSONAL:
ANGELA WATSON　　141

9. TAMING THE BIG EGO　　148

10. GROWING UP　　158

GLOSSARY　　168

RECOMMENDED READING　　171

BIBLIOGRAPHY　　172

## THANK-YOU'S

This book couldn't have been written without the generosity of the many agents, managers, casting directors, producers, and (especially) young actors and their parents who allowed me to talk and spend time with them.  Thank you for sharing your lives with me!  A special thanks to:

The Toovey family, the Hack family, the Sutera family, the Gaines family, the Watson family, the Jensen family, the Richards family, Barbara Babcock, Peter Nelson, Harrison and Marilyn Engel, Terry Ray, Nancy Smith, Jim Stanfield, Nicky Noxon, Judy Belshe, Richard Glasser and family, Wendy Lee, Monika Simmons, Kimberly Johnson, and Paul Petersen.

# RICH, FAMOUS, AND UNDER 18

**S**o you want to be a famous actor—the next Elijah Wood, or Mayim Bialik, or Jonathan Taylor Thomas, or Kellie Martin. You dream of starring in a hit TV show, seeing your name in lights on a movie marquee, and being chased by adoring fans down Hollywood Boulevard. You've got enthusiasm, energy, and a burning desire to make it in show business. There's only one problem. You have absolutely no idea how to make your dream come true.

> When I get all the applause, it's just the best feeling in the world. I love it!
>
> *—Actor Noah Gaines, age twelve*

Relax. All of the young actors you see on TV and in the movies started out just like you—sitting in their living rooms fantasizing about making it big. They

9

didn't have an agent. They didn't have a clue how to get an audition. They didn't even have any acting experience. But somehow they all made the move from unknown hopefuls to popular, working actors.

How did they do it? There are as many answers as there are young stars. Some began their careers as models. Others started in commercials or regional theater. Some struggled for years doing local commercials in small cities before hitting the big time. A few became overnight sensations without having a bit of acting experience.

But despite their different backgrounds, there are a few things that all the young actors you see on TV and in the movies have in common. Can you guess what they are?

The character look sells: Phillip Glasser has acted in plays, movies, television shows, and in hundreds of commercials.

## It Ain't Necessarily So

If you guessed a gorgeous face and a beautiful body, you're wrong. Sure, *Fresh Prince of Bel-Air* star Tatyana Ali and *seaQuest DSV* heartthrob Jonathan Brandis are easy on the eyes. But there are lots of jobs available for less-than-perfect-looking kids. Listen to Kimberly Johnson, a talent agent at the Robert Black Agency in Tempe, Arizona: "People like kids in all shapes and sizes. You don't necessarily have to be a beautiful child in order to get work. Clients now want to see kids as kids. They want to see the child's personality."

Wendy Lee, a talent agent at the Donna Baldwin Talent Agency in Denver, Colorado, says, "I'm always looking for character types. We just signed a boy, he's eight years old. He has carrot-colored hair, freckles, and he weighs about 110 pounds. He's already gotten two local commercials."

Another misconception people have about young stars is that they all grew up in Los Angeles or New York and landed their first job through connections. Not so. Sure, it doesn't hurt to have famous friends and relatives. But there are plenty of current stars who began with no connections and no reason to think they might ever work in Hollywood.

Jonathan Brandis, for example, grew up in Danbury, Connecticut, where his father was a fire fighter. Hilary Swank, star of the movie *The Next Karate Kid,* started her career in Bellingham, Washington. And Luke Perry grew up in Fredericktown, Ohio. None of them had relatives in show business.

Another fallacy is that you can't land a paying acting job until you've had years of acting lessons. In fact, some people will tell you the competition for parts is so stiff that you can't possibly succeed unless you're a "triple threat"—an actor, a singer, *and* a dancer. Certainly that was true fifty years ago. Child stars such as Mickey Rooney, Judy Garland, and Shirley Temple could tap dance, belt out a show tune, tell a joke, and handle dramatic roles with equal skill.

These days, however, kids with little or no training still have a shot at the big time. Just look at Brad Renfro, star of the movie *The Client*. When director Joel Schumacher was searching for a tough, street-smart kid with an authentic Southern accent to play the lead role in the film, he called on casting director Mali Finn. She contacted churches, alternative schools, and police departments in eight Southern cities, looking for the perfect kid. A Knoxville, Tennessee, policeman told her about Brad, who had performed in a school play sponsored by the antidrug organization D.A.R.E.

"He was mesmerizing," says Finn, who interviewed about fifteen hundred boys for the role. "From the second he walked in, I had the feeling this was it." Schumacher agreed and cast Brad in the role. Overnight, Brad Renfro went from being an ordinary kid to being a Hollywood movie star.

Eddie Furlong provides another example. He was only thirteen when a casting director spotted him sitting on the steps of the Boys Club in Pasadena, California, and picked him to star in *Terminator 2*. Within months, his face was plastered across movie posters and magazine covers.

People also make the mistake of thinking that acting talent is hereditary. But even if the rest of your family is too shy to answer the front door, you might still have what it takes to make it in show business. "A lot of families have ten kids, and only one of them becomes famous," says Hollywood casting director Judy Belshe. "It depends on the child's talent and drive . . . it depends on what makes them feel most alive."

*Blossom* star Joey Lawrence sums it up this way: "I don't know where my brothers and I got our talent. My father can't act at all."

Okay, so you don't have to be beautiful or have talented parents, you don't have to live in Los Angeles or New York, you don't need connections, you don't even have to have a lot of experience. Then what exactly *do* you need to make it as a young actor today?

## Where There's a Will, There's a Way

First and foremost, you've got to want to be an actor more than anything else in the world—enough to keep trying despite dozens of rejections. Enough to give up other activities you might enjoy—running for student council or going out for sports, for example—if they interfere with auditions or acting jobs.

Amanda Soden is a fifteen-year-old amateur actress who lives in Santa Barbara, California. Her dream is to star on Broadway. "I want to be one of the big stars, because I know I've got it," she declares. "My mom teases me about the light that comes onto my face when I'm onstage. I love it!"

Chris Demetral, who plays Jeremy on HBO's *Dream On,* told *16,* "I always talked about getting into acting—before I can even remember. My mom said my dream—at age two—was to be on *The Johnny Carson Show.*"

Luke Perry, star of *Beverly Hills 90210,* never

considered any other occupation. "From the time I laid eyes on television for the first time, I had the acting bug," he says. "I was just amazed at what came out of that little box."

Eight-year-old Robyn Richards, who plays Maxie on *General Hospital,* knows what it means to sacrifice for her dreams. Her mother explains: "She'll have plans to go to a birthday party, and at three o'clock I'll pick her up at school and say, 'Robyn, you have to go to L.A.' It hurts for awhile. I say, 'Do you want to do this?' So far, she's always chosen to act."

If you adore acting and can't think of anything else you would rather do with your life, then you've passed the first test.

## A High Ham Quotient

Do you love an audience? Do you make your classmates crack up when you imitate the principal? Does your imitation of Fred Flintstone or the kid on the Eggo Waffles commercial knock 'em dead? Do you adore being the center of attention? If you can answer yes to one or more of these questions, you may have what it takes to be a star.

Even before Robyn Richards became a working actor, she loved to perform. "She was always a ham," her mother remembers. "We were in Disneyland one time and a Dixieland band was playing and Robyn was dancing." She must have had star power even then, because a Disneyland video crew filmed her and asked her mother's permission to use the footage in a promotional video.

Devon Odessa, who played Sharon on *My So-Called Life,* told *16,* "When I lived in West Virginia, I used to mimic commercials in front of my mirror."

Although Luke Perry didn't land his first professional job until he finished high school, he always loved performing. "He would just sing, dance, or do impressions at the drop of a hat," his mother recalls.

If that sounds like you, read on.

## Think Fast!

Are you a good reader? At auditions you will be handed "sides" (pages of the script that contain only the lines of a specific character's role) and be expected to read them out loud with lots of feeling. Usually, you'll have five or ten minutes to prepare before you have to perform. Other times you'll be expected to do a "cold" reading—a reading with no rehearsal at all. If you can read out loud without tripping over the words, you'll do fine.

Later, if you land the part, you'll be expected to read the entire script, figure out your character, and bring him or her to life. According to casting director Judy Belshe, successful young actors have "the ability to take a script, look at it, and turn it into a living, breathing character."

Successful young actors are also good at taking direction. They listen carefully to what the director wants, and they know how to use their voice and their body language to suggest what their character is thinking and feeling. "They're just so aware of themselves and who they are, the image they're presenting, and how they're fitting into their environment," explains Ed Ims, director of the National Association of Showbiz Kids, a nonprofit organization that runs workshops for aspiring child actors.

If you're a good reader and a quick study, and you can follow orders, you've got what it takes to make it in show business.

## Hurry Up and Wait

Acting involves long stretches of sitting around and doing nothing. If you're filming a TV show or a movie, you'll spend a lot of time waiting while the crew arranges the props, sets up the lights, talks to the extras, and does a hundred other little things that must be finished before the director can yell, "Action!"

Even when the camera finally starts rolling, don't expect things to move quickly. Olivia Hack is an twelve-year-old actor with over thirty commercials on her resume. One of her first jobs was a commercial for Socrates, a kids' computer game. Because the sound crew kept goofing up, she was forced to sit under hot lights singing the same jingle over and over and over again. Her experience isn't unusual. "You have to be able to do thirty takes if that's what's required," she says with a shrug.

Do you have plenty of patience? If your answer is yes, you've got the right attitude to be an actor.

## Gimme That Baby Face

You'll have a leg up on the competition if you look younger than you really are. There's nothing a casting director likes better than a child who has the face and body of a six-year-old, but the brains and maturity of a ten-year-old.

Just look at Shawn Toovey, star of *Dr. Quinn,*

*Medicine Woman.* He's twelve but looks younger. "I don't like being tiny," he says, "but it turns out to be a good thing in acting. I can play eight- or nine-year-olds, but I'm old enough that I can learn the lines and handle the business."

Another example is Damon Giannatassio, a model and actor from Atlanta, Georgia. Damon was born with a growth disorder. When he was nine years old, he won a statewide modeling search. According to Eva Stancil, coauthor of *Kids on Camera,* one of the judges on the panel had this to say about Damon: "There he was, at least five inches shorter than the other nine-year-olds. He was adorable because he looked so much younger but acted so much older. I personally felt that he could take on many different types of modeling jobs, particularly those requiring a boy around five or six. I felt he could handle it with the maturity of a nine-year-old."

If you're sick of being teased because you're small for your age, acting could be a way to make your size work to your advantage.

## Reality Check

To be a successful child star, you must have the ability to turn on emotions at the drop of a hat, and turn them off just as quickly. One minute you're being asked to pretend your parents were just eaten by aliens from the planet Zorb; the next minute the director is yelling, "Cut! Let's break for lunch!"

Robyn Richards remembers a scene from *General Hospital* in which her character, Maxie, learned that the new heart she'd received in a transplant operation originally belonged to her recently deceased cousin.

Robyn Richards can turn on the tears when the director yells "Action!" and smile when he yells "Cut!"

"Robyn cried on cue," her mother recalls, "but when it was over, she could laugh."

Shawn Toovey had a similar experience when he played the son of a town bully in a TV movie. "He had a scene where he had to be really emotional," his mother says. "His pa had died, his pet was dead. We got such a kick out of watching him because he'd do the scene, and the minute they yelled 'Cut!' he'd be smiling and playing games."

Can you laugh and cry on cue? That's a plus!

## Calm, Cool, and Collected

Young actors have to be comfortable relating to strangers, especially adult strangers. "Shy is really tough to deal with," explains talent agent Wendy Lee. "They [shy kids] are not going to be able to stand in front of a complete stranger and do what he tells them to do."

Kimberly Johnson, a talent agent at the Robert Black Agency, agrees. "You need to be open enough to be comfortable relating to someone you don't know. I tell the parents that you can be there [at an audition or on the set] but the child has to be able to say, 'Okay, Mom, I'm going to go with these people now.' No matter how cute the kid is, if they can't talk to me or if they freak out when their parents leave, it's not going to work."

Robyn Richards proved from the start that she could perform in front of strangers. When she had her first interview with a potential agent, she was asked to pretend she was eating an ice-cream cone. Robyn threw herself into the fantasy without a bit of self-consciousness. "I pretended I was eating chocolate ice cream," she says, "and I asked for a napkin." The agent signed her on the spot.

Could you do what Robyn did? If it sounds easy, you may have acting in your blood.

### Rhinoceros Skin

It takes a thick skin to survive in show business. Every time you go to an audition, you're allowing other people to judge you. When they say no, it can hurt.

Listen to Jan Carter, director of the Santa Barbara (California) Children's Theater: "The child will be there [at an audition] all prepped and ready to go. He'll open his mouth and say the first line of three or four pages they gave him, and if they don't like it, they'll say, 'Thank you. Good-bye.'"

Sometimes they reject you even sooner. Noah

Gaines, a twelve-year-old actor who has appeared in over twenty regional theater productions, describes his experiences at a "cattle call" (open audition) in Los Angeles: "They take in maybe six kids at a time, and sometimes they only have two kids read and they say, 'Okay, that's all we need. Good-bye.' And the other four kids leave without opening their mouths. It's very frustrating!"

Mea Hack, mother of Olivia Hack, puts it this way: "It's a real training ground for life. It's okay if the kid has the kind of personality that can take it."

Can you take it? If you can shrug off rejection and try, try again, then you've got what it takes to succeed.

## That Certain Something

The final characteristic needed to be a successful child actor cannot be bought, borrowed, or learned. You're either born with it or you're not. Some call it natural talent, some call it star quality, some call it charisma. Whatever label you put on it, it's the ability to hold an audience spellbound, to make people *want* to watch you perform.

Listen to Eva Stancil, owner/director of Kiddin' Around Models And Talent in Atlanta, Georgia. "To call a kid a natural is always a great compliment," she says in her book *Kids on Camera*. "Generally, it refers to a child who doesn't get inhibited in front of people or the camera, who instinctively moves well and who follows directions easily."

Television producer Irene Dreayer told *People* how she felt when she first met Tia and Tamera Mowry: "They were so adorable, I wanted to go hang out at the mall with them." She was so impressed by their charisma that she created the TV series *Sister, Sister* for them to star in.

Have you ever heard the phrase "the camera loves him"? It's used to describe a person who looks terrific in photographs and on film. A perfect example is Brad Renfro. "He was very charismatic," Mali Finn says, describing their first meeting. "He had a face that people could watch for two hours. His eyes were extraordinary."

You can't decide for yourself if you have charisma. It's something other people will see and comment on. If they do—repeatedly and enthusiastically—consider yourself extremely lucky. You've got that special *something* that separates the ordinary people from the superstars.

## THREE REALLY BAD REASONS FOR GETTING INTO SHOW BUSINESS

**1.** *You think acting will make you rich.*

In *The Young Performer's Guide,* Barbara Elman Schiffman states: "There are over eight thousand Screen Actors Guild members under eighteen, with about 15% earning top dollar; the rest audition a lot and work occasionally . . ."

Of course, it *is* possible to earn a lot of money fast—sometimes for surprisingly little work. Talent agent Wendy Lee tells the story of a child who landed a role in a Boston Chicken commercial. "He's not even recognizable—you see the back of his head—but he makes probably a thousand dollars a month in residuals [a royalty which is paid to the performer each time the commercial is aired]."

Think of it this way: in show business, as in life,

you should hope for the best and expect the worst. Acting could make you rich . . . but don't count on it.

**2.** *You think acting will make you famous.*

Jonathan Brandis receives four thousand fan letters a week. Joey Lawrence gets mobbed at shopping malls. But for every famous heartthrob, there are tens of thousands of kids simply trying to get work. Jan Carter, director of the Santa Barbara Children's Theater, says, "We've probably had fifteen kids in the last twenty years who have gotten one Hollywood job. Of those, maybe three have gotten something big out of it."

Even if you *do* get work as an actor, don't think you'll automatically have fans falling at your feet. "I get teased a lot," Noah Gaines admits. He remembers when he was acting in a play and had a break between performances. His mother made him go to school—with his stage makeup on. "The next day I got lipstick left in my locker," he says with a sigh.

Fame is fine, but if you're going to act, do it because you love it. As *Fresh Prince* star Alfonso Ribeiro says, "You can't do it because you want to be a star . . . you can't do it for the limelight and the people loving you. You have to want to be an actor."

**3.** *You think acting is glamorous and fun.*

Sure, acting can be a thrill. But it's also hard work. "I never had any misconceptions that it was all glamorous," Brian Gaskill of *Models Inc.* told *Bop*. "It is all work!" Still, he adds, "The scripts are a lot of fun and I like doing it."

"The hardest thing for me is giving up my social

life," Joanna Hayes says in *Kids on Camera*. "When I was doing my play [the musical *Annie*], I would go to bed at 2:30 A.M. and have to wake up at 6:00 A.M. Sometimes that would leave me with only having two hours of sleep every night."

If acting is your dream, you'll love every minute it. But if you think performing is a way to get out of school and goof off, you're in for a big surprise. Elijah Wood summed up the life of a child star in *16*: "Kids fantasize about being actors. Everyone thinks it's glamorous. But it's a lot of hard work."

# Up Close and Personal:

## Shawn Toovey

Most of the actors you see on television have spent years struggling to get where they are. But for eleven-year-old Shawn Toovey, it was just a hop, skip, and a jump from total obscurity in San Antonio, Texas, to national fame on the CBS television series *Dr. Quinn, Medicine Woman*. How'd he do it? Read on.

Shawn was born in Nebraska and spent the first five years of his life on the move. His father, Jim, was a trucker who owned his own rig, and young Shawn traveled in the cab with his parents. "I've logged like five hundred thousand miles in a truck," he proclaims.

When it was time to start school, the family settled in San Antonio, where his mother decided to teach him at home. At that point, acting was the furthest thing from Shawn's mind. He did, however, take tap and jazz dance lessons. "I used to roll up the rug in the living room and dance to Michael Jackson music," he says with a laugh.

Shawn Toovey

Shawn's parents were complete strangers to show business, but despite that, their son did get some early acting training. "I'm a dramatic person," his mother, Cynthia, explains. When she read stories to him, she acted out the parts, using different voices and lots of expression. "Then Shawn started doing that, too," she says.

But it was Shawn's looks, not his acting ability, that helped him land his first job when he was only six years old. "My mom and I were walking through the mall one day and a lady came out of a store and asked me if I wanted to do some freeze modeling," Shawn says. (Freeze models are models who stand in store windows, pretending to be mannequins.) "I liked doing it," he says, "so I asked my mom to get me an agent." (An agent helps actors and models find jobs.)

How did Mom and Dad react? "They had their doubts at first," Shawn admits. "I think they figured 'Well, let's see where it leads.' They pretty much go with the flow."

It didn't take long for Shawn to get an agent. "A friend of mine told me about an agent in San Antonio," his mother explains. "She said all you do is take a photograph and send it in. The agent said she wanted to meet Shawn, so we went in for an interview. She liked him and sent him to a modeling seminar."

The seminar taught Shawn how to move on a modeling runway and in front of a camera. Soon he was doing runway modeling around San Antonio. Then, one day, a casting director from ABC came to town. She was checking out the local talent and making file tapes (short videotaped auditions) of child actors for possible use in the future.

"They had me read a paragraph out of a book of *Snow White*," Shawn remembers. The casting director must have liked his performance because she showed the tape to her friend Lee Peterson, a manager (a person who guides an actor's career) in Houston.

Peterson remembers that day well. "The ABC casting agent called me and said, 'I want you to meet this kid. He's really got potential, and I think he's the kind of child you want to work with.'"

Peterson decided to meet with Shawn in person. "I really liked Cynthia, and immediately I connected with Shawn," she says. "He had a lot of charisma. And he was examining me as much as I was examining him. I loved it! That kind of behavior in a child lets you know he's very bright and isn't intimidated by adults."

At first, Shawn's parents were a little leery of signing with a manager. Modeling had been just a hobby for Shawn, but Peterson wanted to send him to acting auditions. Mr. and Mrs. Toovey thought it over, spoke with Shawn (who was eager to try his hand at acting), and checked out Peterson's credentials. Finally, they decided to sign on the dotted line.

After that, things happened fast. Within the month Shawn auditioned for an HBO movie. "I had butterflies in my stomach," he recalls. "They had three or four people there, and they had me read from the script. Then they had me go and see the director." A few days later, Shawn was offered the part. He was ecstatic—until he saw the script. His part contained obscene language. He took one look at it and said, "I'm not saying that!"

Shawn's mother called Peterson, who asked HBO to rewrite the dialogue. They refused, and Peterson encouraged Shawn to turn down the job. For Peterson, the choice was simple. "Shawn has to feel good about what he does," she explains. "We deal with the human element first, and that means he has to be happy." Besides, she felt confident Shawn would get another chance at stardom soon.

She was right. Later that same month he auditioned for an NBC television movie, *In Broad Daylight,* and was offered the part. He was cast as the son of a town bully, played by Brian Dennehy. "I was nervous at first," Shawn remembers. "*Very* nervous." To make matters worse, Shawn was surprised to learn that movies aren't filmed in chronological order. "Sometimes they'd do my scene . . . then skip a scene . . . then my scene, my scene, then skip a scene," he explains. "But after a while I sort of got into the rhythm. The story sucked me in."

Shawn must have pulled it off because after that, he landed roles in three more TV movies. But that doesn't mean there weren't setbacks. "I've done lots of auditions where I didn't get the part," he points out. Fortunately, he doesn't let rejection get him down. "If it's a movie I really, really, *really* want, I feel a little bad . . . but it's not that big a deal. If I get it, I get it . . . if not, oh well."

Then, in 1992, Shawn was selected to play the role of Brian Cooper in the *Dr. Quinn, Medicine Woman* pilot. When CBS decided to add the show to its fall lineup, Shawn and his family rented a furnished apartment near the Paramount Ranch in the Santa Monica Mountains, where the series is filmed. Suddenly, Shawn was a full-time actor. But what he didn't realize was that the series would be a hit—and he would become a star.

"It's starting to sink in," he admits. "I just learned they're going to make *Dr. Quinn* action figures. When I heard that, it sort of hit me—wow!"

Another indication that Shawn has become a celebrity is the fan mail he receives. And, of course, people are starting to recognize him on the street. "It used to be that people said, 'You look just like the boy on the *Dr. Quinn* show,'" his mother says. "But yesterday someone said, 'You're Shawn Toovey!'"

Then there was the time he and his mother were staying in a hotel in San Antonio and he was spotted by a choral group that was in town for a competition. "They swarmed our room," Cynthia remembers. "There must have been thirty people who came in, and they all wanted autographs."

"It was fun at first," Shawn admits, "but after awhile of signing and signing, it got old. But I haven't done it quite enough times to be tired of it."

Fortunately, none of the adulation has given Shawn a swelled head. He's still the same person he was before the series began—a devoted *Star Trek* fan who enjoys reading *Disney Adventures,* playing baseball, and hanging out with his old friends from San Antonio. "They [his friends] are excited to know someone who's on a series," Shawn's mother says, "but they don't talk about it. They just go play."

But when the series is being filmed, Shawn's visits to San Antonio are few and far between. His shooting schedule changes every week, depending on how many scenes he's in. Sometimes he starts work at dawn; other days he doesn't arrive on the set until dusk. There isn't time to go to a regular school, so he's tutored three hours a day on the set.

Although Shawn loves being an actor, he says filming *Dr. Quinn* is not all fun and games. Sometimes the temperature on the set gets up to 115 degrees—hard to take when you're filming a Christmas show in heavy woolen clothing! At other times, the cast has had to contend with rain, hail, and even floods. "We were filming during the floods of '92," Shawn recalls. "One day we were just getting ready to rehearse, and the park ranger came up and said, 'You have forty-five minutes to get changed and get out of here, or you're probably going to be stuck.'" Fortunately, Shawn and his family did escape, but they had to take a last-minute detour to avoid a mud slide!

On the up side, Shawn's experience on *Dr. Quinn* has given him a chance to fine-tune his acting ability. One of the most difficult skills for many child actors to master is crying on cue. Last year Shawn decided to give it a try.

"It was during a scene in the Halloween show," he explains. "The script never said I had to cry. I just thought that might be the way Brian would have felt, so I asked the director if maybe I could try it in the shot. I waited until they were setting up the lights," he continues. "No one was bothering me, so I just stood by myself and thought about what I wanted to do." What exactly did he think about? "I've never revealed that information," he says with a mysterious smile. "It's like a magician's trick—it's my secret."

What does the future hold for Shawn Toovey? Sometimes he pictures himself leaving show business behind. "I've never gotten to be in Little League," he says wistfully. "When this series is over, I might decide to play a little baseball and go to high school." At other times, he dreams of acting in feature films or in the theater. He might even enjoy directing someday. But no matter what the future holds for Shawn, there's one thing for certain—he isn't going to turn into a Hollywood brat. "I'm just going to keep learning and growing," he declares. "It's cool to see yourself on TV, but I'm just somebody who got lucky."

Maybe. But it takes talent, desire, and a lot of hard work to turn a lucky break into a career. And Shawn Toovey's career is really taking off.

# CHAPTER 2

# STARTING SMALL

**O**kay, you've made up your mind. You want to be an actor, and you're willing to work to make it happen. What do you do next?

Listen to top Hollywood talent agent J. Michael Bloom: "Training is the most important thing," he told K Callan in *The Los Angeles Agent Book.* "I get very annoyed with people. Someone is attractive, so people say, 'You should be in television,' and then the actor just thinks that's going to just happen."

If you're going to be in the communications business, you need to watch all the time how people are communicating.

*—Casting director Judy Belshe*

Even a so-called "natural" like Brad Renfro didn't step into his role in *The Client* without training. After he was cast, the film studio sent him to a Hollywood acting coach for lessons. And when Steven Spielberg selected Christian Bale out of four thousand talented hopefuls to play the lead in *Empire of the Sun,* it wasn't just because of the boy's charisma. According to *Newsweek,* ". . . his Oscar-caliber performance—in which he grows from a snotty schoolboy to a savvy, hollow-eyed black marketeer—was doubtlessly helped by his training."

If you don't have the money to take acting lessons from a famous Hollywood teacher, don't sweat it. You can get the beginning acting experience you need absolutely free, right in your own hometown. "They [aspiring young actors] need to get involved in school

Noah Gaines (far right) rehearses a dance number for the musical *Bizzy!*

plays and church plays," urges casting director Nancy Smith. "Audition for local theater, and if there are any children's theater groups in your area, definitely get involved with them."

But what if you try out for the school play and don't land a part? "If you can't get an acting job," casting director Judy Belshe says, "take a job doing the lighting or the painting. Every job you do increases your knowledge and decreases your anxiety. When you see [other actors] make mistakes, you realize these people aren't perfect. You can do it."

Don't be afraid to start small. "I started in summer children's theater," Noah Gaines says. "The first couple times I was, like, the lowest of the low—I played a little squirrel or a little cookie man in *Hansel and Gretel*. Then one summer I got a semi-lead, and I was so excited. And every summer I worked my way up."

## To Study or Not to Study

If you've acted in a few school plays or church pageants but haven't received any formal training, it might be time to consider some acting lessons. Many schools offer drama or public-speaking courses. Also check out your local community center, Girls Club or Boys Club, and Parks and Recreation Department. These groups often give free acting workshops or at least offer scholarships for low-income kids.

If you have to pay to take acting lessons, make sure they're worth the money. "If it's over two hundred dollars and it's less than six weeks, it's a rip-off," says Judy Belshe. "That's my rule of thumb." Also, check out the teacher's credentials. Does he or she have any professional acting credits? How many years has he been teaching? Does she belong to the Organization of Professional Acting Coaches and Teachers? What do his former students say about the course?

In *The Young Performer's Guide,* New York acting teacher Rita Litton urges beginning actors to train in a class with other students, rather than signing up with an acting coach for one-on-one sessions. "If the coach, often a former actor or actress, is working opposite you in a scene, he or she is *acting* with you, and is not able to truly watch and judge *your* performance," she explains.

## The More the Merrier

Just because you think you want to be an actor doesn't mean you should spend every waking moment acting. There are many, many other talents you can develop that will help you in your acting career *and* put you in front of people—talents such as dancing, singing, gymnastics, juggling, playing an instrument . . . the list is practically endless.

Many famous working actors didn't start out in acting. Carol Ann Planté, who has acted on Broadway and on the TV series *Harry and the Hendersons,* began as a baton twirler. Hilary Swank, star of *The Next Karate Kid,* competed in gymnastics and swimming in the Junior Olympics when she was fourteen. "My flexibility from gymnastics and the strength from swimming came together in this film," she told *16.*

Claire Danes, who played Angela on *My So-Called Life,* began modern dance lessons at age six. And Marques Houston performed in a rap group before he was picked to play Tia and Tamera's next-door neighbor on the TV series *Sister, Sister.*

So don't think acting is the only way to go. The main thing is to perform. Casting director Nancy Smith agrees. "Get involved with cheerleading, baton twirling, dancing, anything that puts you in front of people," she urges. "You need the experience of being in front of an audience without freezing."

## Learning the Biz

Acting lessons will teach you the basic principles of performing onstage, and acting in local theater will give you a chance to try out your new-found skills. But how will you learn what it takes to find an agent or to land a role in a commercial or a feature film?

If you live in or near a large city, you can take a workshop or seminar run by show business professionals. Different workshops will teach you different things—how to act in commercials, how to find an agent, how to get into modeling. Others will give you an overview of the entire industry.

Even working actors attend workshops and seminars. Joanna Hayes is an eleven-year-old model and actress who has appeared in nine plays and thirteen TV commercials. "I think you can never get enough training," she says in the book *Kids on Camera.* "Each time I take a workshop I feel like I am learning more. It helps you at being more professional, and you have a better chance of getting more auditions because of what you have learned."

Sometimes show business workshops are run by talent agents, managers, casting directors, or modeling agencies who are searching for new talent.

Paul Sutera (*The Brady Bunch Movie*), for example, was discovered by manager Gary Scalzer at a workshop in Orlando, Florida.

How do you know which workshops are legitimate and which are only seeking to separate you from your money? As with acting classes, check out the credentials of the people running the workshops. Are they professionals? Exactly what jobs have they held in the industry? Ask for references and check up on them. Call the Better Business Bureau to see if they've had any complaints.

Be extremely wary of any workshop or class advertised with the promise that it's easy to make it in show business. It isn't, and if their ad says that, the people running the workshop are probably trying to take you for a ride. "You'll get the Hollywood line," warns former child star Paul Petersen. "I caution you to ask yourself, 'Where do these people make their money?'"

Remember, if an acting or modeling workshop promises to find you an agent or guarantees to get you work, run—don't walk—to the nearest exit. As acting teacher Rita Litton writes in *The Young Performer's Guide,* "No acting school should—or can!—promise you work."

Watch out for companies that publish books containing photographs of aspiring actors. These businesses promise to circulate their book to important Hollywood producers, directors, and casting directors. But show business professionals hire actors through talent agents, not by glancing through books of photographs.

"A lot of companies come through town and say 'we do commercials and modeling, come listen to our lecture,'" warns Nancy Smith. "Then they say you can be in their book, but you have to pay three hundred dollars. That's a big scam."

## *Do It Yourself*

You say your parents can't (or won't) pay for acting lessons? Don't give up! There are plenty of things you can learn about acting without the aid of a teacher. For starters, you can watch other actors and learn from them. If there are any free theater performances in your area, go to them. When you attend a school play, observe your fellow students closely. What makes some actors mesmerizing and others just so-so? Take notes.

Watch TV shows and movies with a new eye. Instead of letting yourself get caught up in the story, step back and watch the acting. How does Ethan Hawke use body language to express his character's inner feelings? Why does Julia Roberts seem so lovable on screen? What does Elijah Wood do when the other characters in the movie are speaking?

Rent videos and watch cable TV to see classic movies. Check out the films of famous child stars from the past—kids like Shirley Temple, Jackie Coogan, Mickey Rooney, Judy Garland, and Freddie Bartholomew. Watch Henry Thomas in *E.T.,* Tatum O'Neal in *Paper Moon,* and Drew Barrymore in *Irreconcilable Differences.* Memorize your favorite scenes and practice them in front of the mirror.

Go to the library and check out some books on acting. Read star biographies and autobiographies, books on acting methods, and books about the business side of show business. Learn what happens behind the scenes—how a movie is made, what a cinematographer does, the details of a stage manager's job. Read plays and screenplays, too. Study the history of theater, cinema, radio, and television.

Check out books of scenes and monologues. Learn a monologue and perform it—first, in front of the mirror; then, for your family and friends. Practice acting out scenes with friends who are also aspiring actors. Put on a play in your neighborhood. If it goes over well, ask your church, community center, or local daycare center if you can perform it for them.

Talk to working actors. Whenever you get a chance to see a professional or semiprofessional play, go backstage after the performance and ask if you can meet the actors. Ask them how they got started. Tell them you want to be an actor, and ask for their advice.

Film actor Mary Steenburgen will never forget seeing *The Music Man* and *South Pacific* when she was a child. "Those plays changed my life—I couldn't stop thinking about them," she says in the *Los Angeles Times*. "And when I met one of the actors in *South Pacific* and he said, 'Look at that little girl's eyes—there's an actress in there,' I loved it so much I could barely breathe."

## From Your Town to Hollywood

If you've got stars in your eyes and Hollywood in your heart, acting in school plays and local theater may seem like small potatoes. Wrong. Many working actors started out exactly that way.

Just look at fourteen-year-old film star Tom Guiry. "I went to an audition for *A Christmas Carol* at the McCarter Theater [in Princeton, New Jersey]. I got it

Phillip Glasser played the role of Gavroch in the Los Angeles production of *Les Miserables*.

and a casting director spotted me, then I went to an agent in New York City, then I got *The Sandlot*."

Casting director Nancy Smith is always looking for kids who have theater experience. "I go to a lot of children's shows, so I see a lot of kids, and I know what they can do," she says. "I would never send anyone without experience out on a speaking part."

And remember, acting isn't the only way to showcase your talents. Any kind of performance will work. The idea is to get yourself in front of people.

"I was five years old and I was taking baton lessons with my older sister, Carla," Carol Ann Planté says in the video *Modeling, Commercials & Acting.* "The baton teacher sent me on an audition for a play called *Gypsy*, and I got the part. I started doing theater productions . . . I did about forty plays."

Eventually, she landed a role in *The Marriage of Figaro* on Broadway.

Mario Lopez (*Saved by the Bell*) took dance lessons as a child. He was at a dance contest in San Diego, California, when a casting agent spotted him and asked him to audition for the TV series *AKA Pablo*.

When he was ten years old, Brian Austin Green (*Beverly Hills 90210*) went to a performing arts school on the University of Southern California campus. He acted in movies produced by students in the USC film program and eventually used his work in those films to land a Hollywood agent.

Brian cautions beginning actors to do their best in every job, even the amateur ones. "When you're first starting out, don't take it like '. . . this is stupid. I don't want to do this,'" he says in *Modeling, Commercials & Acting*. "Take it like 'Okay, let's see how much I can learn today.'"

## TEN FUN, FREE WAYS TO PRACTICE YOUR ACTING SKILLS

**1.** *Start a liar's club.* Sit around with your friends and take turns telling stories—some true, some outrageous whoppers. Practice keeping a straight face and speaking with total sincerity. When each kid finishes his story, the others can try to guess whether it was the truth or a lie. The kid who stumps the most people wins.

**2.** *Practice improvising with other aspiring actors.* Write several interesting situations on pieces of paper and put them in a hat. Then choose a piece of paper and act out the scene. A sample scene: A kid walks into McDonald's with a three-hundred-pound pig and orders lunch. One actor can play the part of the pig owner, one can be a McDonald's employee, and one can play the pig. Start acting and see what happens.

**3.** *Watch the people around you closely.* How do they walk, talk, move their hands, laugh, frown? What makes them different from each other? Practice mimicking their voices and body language in front of the mirror.

**4.** *Think about the funniest thing that ever happened to you.* Practice laughing in a believable way. Now remember the saddest thing that ever happened to you. Can you make yourself cry?

**5.** *Get your hands on a book of monologues and scenes.* Memorize a monologue and practice performing it in front of the mirror. Act it out for your family or friends.

**6.** *Create a character who is the same age as you but comes from a different family and town.* Imagine your pretend family, your house, your school, your friends, and your neighborhood. Create some unique body language for your character, a style of dress, a way of speaking. Practice being your character. Go into a store and ask directions in the way your character would.

**7.** *Pick a character you enjoyed in a movie, TV show, or play and pretend you are that character.* Imagine yourself in different situations (in a fight, lost in a strange city, as a new kid in school). How would your character act?

**8.** *Put on a neighborhood play.* Get your friends together and write a play. Make the scenery, find the props, create the costumes. Post signs in the neighborhood advertising your play. Put on one or more performances.

**9.** *Think of five different ways to show various emotions.* What kind of body language could you use to show that you're angry, sad, frustrated, or bored? Share your ideas with friends and act them out.

**10.** *Imagine what the life of a movie character was like before the movie began.* What happened to him after the movie ended? Act out scenes from your prologue and sequel.

# CHAPTER  3

# MOM, CAN I BE A SUPERSTAR?

**Y**ou've got the desire to be a star. You've got the talent. You've got the drive. Why do you need your parents' help? Why can't you just go for it?

If you're too young to drive a car, the answer is obvious. How are you going to get to auditions by yourself? Even if you live in a city with good public transportation, you'll have a tough time. Sometimes auditions are held in out-of-the-way places. Mea Hack, mother of eleven-year-old actress Olivia Hack, remembers

> Robyn and I make the car ride to L.A. exciting so she doesn't get bored. We're not doing it just for the money. It has to be fun.
>
> —*Mary Richards,*
> *Robyn Richards's mother*

Olivia Hack and her mother, Mea (right), chat with the author outside the family's Los Angeles home

when her daughter auditioned for *The Lion King*. "It was in the middle of nowhere, in an industrial park," she says. "We drove past it nine times."

Even if you have your license and the use of the family car, you still need your parents' cooperation for legal reasons. In most parts of the country, underage actors must have a valid work permit. To get one, you need your parents' permission. A parent or legal guardian is also required to sign your contracts. No contract, no job.

But there's an even more important reason why you need to get your parents involved in your career. Acting is a demanding, competitive business. You need all the support you can get. Your parents—in fact, your entire family—should be your biggest fans, the ones who cheer the loudest when you land a role and hug you the tightest when you blow an audition. If your parents and siblings are criticizing your acting and saying "I told you so" every time you fail, it's going to make it twice as hard for you to handle the ups and downs of show business.

Malcolm-Jamal Warner (*The Cosby Show*) knows how important it is to have a supportive family. "An important part of my life, and of my career as well, is my mom, Pamela Warner," he says in *The Young Performer's Guide*. "She always has been and always will be in my corner. . . . She's my mother, manager, business partner, and best friend. I have the security of knowing that she will always be there to watch my back."

## That Special Someone

What if your parents approve of your budding career, but neither Mom nor Dad has the time it takes to get actively involved? Don't give up! All you need is a responsible adult who has been appointed by your parents. It could be an aunt or uncle, an older brother or sister (as long as they are over eighteen), a grandparent, or even a family friend or neighbor. If you can find a grown-up who is willing to accompany you to auditions and jobs—*and* your parents approve— you're in business.

## What's in It for Me?

Why would someone want to be a stage parent? For starters, it's fun. Imagine getting a chance to hang around a movie set, meet famous stars, and watch your child perform with them. "I'm a stay-home mom," says Laura Jensen, mother of five young models and actors. "This adds a little interest and gets me out of the laundry room."

Second, there's the possibility that your child will make a lot of money. "Money is definitely an issue," says Noah Gaines's mother, Janet. "You think, 'Well, one McDonald's commercial and that could pay for their college education.'"

Some parents also double as their child's manager, and that can make for a thrilling new career. Listen to Tom Chestaro, stepfather and manager of actor Anthony Michael Hall (*Weird Science, The Breakfast Club*): "It's a very exciting business," he says in *The Young Performer's Guide*. "I enjoy working with the producers, the directors, the writers, and the executives. I enjoy learning further about the dynamics of the business."

Finally, being a stage parent is a way for mothers and fathers to help their child's dreams of stardom come true. James Pulliam, whose daughter, Keshia, was on *The Cosby Show,* says in *The Young Performer's Guide:* "I saw it as a chance to give her something most daughters can't get from their fathers." And he adds, "Who knows what's best for Keshia better than I, her father?"

## Mom Is Auditioning, Too

What is expected of the parent or guardian of a working child actor? Plenty! Casting director David Ruben says, "When casting kids, you must be conscious that you're also casting the parents. . . . Producers, directors, and casting people are very aware of the dynamic between the parent and the child, since the parent's going to be on the set a great deal."

Does the supportive adult in your life (referred to

as your stage parent throughout this book) have what it takes to help, not hinder, your acting career? Read on and find out.

## The Clock Is Ticking

First and foremost, it takes time to be a good stage parent. Is your parent or guardian available to drive you to the nearest big city for an audition any day of the week? What if you got a call on Thursday morning for a job that same afternoon? Could your stage parent take you?

"When the agent calls and says you have an audition today at noon, you have to stop everything and get down there," explains Mary Richards, mother of *General Hospital* star Robyn Richards. "Because if you tell them no, they're not going to waste their time on you. They've got other kids who will do it."

If a casting director is considering you for a part, you may be called back to audition again and again. Each time, your stage parent has to be available to drive you. "My mom would drive me back and forth [to auditions], 'cause we lived sixty miles from L.A.," says Wilson Cruz, who played Rickie on *My So-Called Life*.

If you land a modeling or acting job, your stage parent will be expected to be on the set with you the entire time. If you land a full-time job on a series, your stage parent will automatically have a full-time job, too—being on the set with you.

"The parent has to get the big picture," explains casting director Judy Belshe. "The parent has to ask, 'Do I have the support system for this?'"

If your stage parent can answer yes, you're on your way.

## A Family Affair

Do you have brothers and sisters? How will they feel if your stage parent is constantly driving you to auditions? Will they feel left out? What if you land a role in a TV series and become famous? Will they be jealous?

If you have other siblings who are also in show business, things can get even more complicated. Stage mother Mea Hack says, "I know a woman right now who has one child who did a pilot, but the other isn't doing much. You can get these sibling rivalries."

A good stage parent can support your career without neglecting the rest of the family. Joyce Sutera spends six months of the year in Los Angeles with her actor son, Paul, while her husband stays home in Florida with the other children. "My husband learned how to cook and how to do laundry," she says. "It's been good. When we're together, we really enjoy the time. It's been a sacrifice, but it's been kind of fun."

Joyce Sutera works hard to keep the lines of communication open, to give equal attention to everyone in the family, and to make sure no one is feeling jealous or neglected. "Our family talks," she says. "We talk about everything."

If your stage parent can juggle the emotional needs of your family *and* your career, that's a plus.

## Get Organized

Dropping everything and rushing off to an audition is not only time-consuming, it's also crazy-making. Listen to Robyn Richards's mother: "[Sometimes] she'll have three or four auditions a day, plus a script to be taped. And then I'm thinking, 'Okay, is my car packed in case it's late and we have to stay down there? Is Robert [Robyn's brother] taken care of? Where's my husband?' It's hard!"

A good stage parent can handle the pressure. She's organized. She has a book with all her appointments neatly noted in it. She can find her way through busy city streets at rush hour. She remembers to leave a tuna casserole in the fridge for the rest of the family to eat while she's driving you to an audition in a city one hundred miles away.

"I look for a responsible parent who I know I can trust to get their child to a job," says talent agent Wendy Lee. "You get real flaky parents. There's one woman with beautiful children who's really a nightmare. She'll leave a message on my office machine that her car broke down so I get to work and find out they had a call time [the time they were due on the set] at eight o'clock and they never made it. I almost don't want to send her kids' pictures out anymore."

Can your stage parent get you where you need to be, on time, clean, rested, dressed appropriately, and ready to work? If so, there's a good chance you'll succeed.

### Sit Down and Shut Up

Naturally, your mother and father feel they know what's best for you. But at auditions and on modeling and acting jobs, your stage parent will be expected to kept quiet and let other people—the casting director, the director, the makeup artist, the hair stylist, and so on—decide what's best for you.

Stage parents who are pushy on the set are a definite no-no. Talent agent Kimberly Johnson recalls: "I had one mother who got overly concerned with what's going on. It was her child's first job, and she was telling the people [on the set] that she didn't like what they were dressing her daughter in and that they needed to comb her hair a different way!"

On the other hand, your stage parent must speak up if you are being mistreated. For example, Laura Jensen remembers her son Matt's first modeling job: "The lady who was modeling as his mother was quite a little flirt. When Matt went in [to the dressing room] to change his clothes, she walked in there and took off her dress—and she had no bra on!"

When the job was finished, Mrs. Jensen called Matt's agent and complained. The agent assured Mrs. Jensen that the woman would be reported to her agent, and Matt would never have to work with her again.

Knowing when to keep quiet and when to speak up is the sign of a good stage parent.

## Money Madness

Under normal circumstances, kids don't earn more money than their parents do. But show business is not "normal" in this respect. It's possible for you to earn big bucks, and that can mean new responsibilities for your mother and father.

There are laws that govern how much of a working child's income must be put in a trust fund for the child. But the laws vary from state to state, and they only pertain to long-term jobs, such as TV series and movies. Since you are a minor, the money you make

Like father, like son: David Jensen acted in local theater, then his son, Matt, caught the acting bug. Now the whole family is into acting and modeling.

from modeling jobs, commercials, or guest spots on a TV series will be controlled by your parents.

Most stage parents handle their child's money wisely. But a few go a little nuts. Listen to talent agent Wendy Lee: "I have one mother who has the most beautiful little girl . . . we got her a national ad and her mother called me one day and said, 'Now how much am I allowed to spend on myself?' I said she should probably put 50 percent away for her daughter and she said, 'But is there a legal thing?' I think this woman is running out to Neiman-Marcus and spending it all."

The most successful, most well-adjusted child stars come from families that were financially stable *before* the child started acting. In those families, the young actor's salary isn't needed to pay the rent, so it can be kept in trust for the child. Stage mother Laura Jensen says, "My kids have to tithe 10 percent of it to the church, 10 percent they can keep to blow however they want, and the rest of it is saved for college."

## Motivate, Don't Suffocate

Have you ever seen the musical *Gypsy*? It's the story of an overbearing stage mother, one who pushes her children into show business against their will. It's hard to believe, but there are a lot of parents like that out there.

"I see them in auditions," Mary Richards says. "They're constantly fidgeting over their child and the child is saying, 'Mom, I don't want to do it,' and the mother says, 'You have to.'"

If you are reading this book, you probably *want* to be an actor, and your parents aren't forcing you into the business. But even if the original desire to perform was all yours, your parents can still be overbearing.

"Some mothers try to direct the child without having any knowledge of what we're doing in the audition," casting director Annette Stilwell says in *Kids on Camera*. "The mother is prompting the child or even threatening the child. It's amazing and disturbing."

On the other hand, a little gentle prompting isn't bad. Listen to twelve-year-old Noah Gaines: "Sometimes I say, 'I don't want to do this, Mom,' and she says, 'Come on, Noah.' And then I get there and meet the people and get into it and say, 'Yeah, this is cool.' And my mom says, 'What did I tell you, Noah?' I think because I'm a kid, I still need a little pushing."

If your stage parent can motivate you without suffocating you, you'll do just fine.

## SEVEN WAYS TO CONVINCE YOUR PARENTS TO LET YOU BE AN ACTOR

What if your parents are dead set against you being in show business? How can you convince them that you need their support? Here are some tips that have worked for other kids:

**1.** *Don't expect your parents to pick up and move to Hollywood just because you've decided you want to be a star.* You have to prove to them you're serious by successfully landing some local jobs. Hilary Swank got her start acting in plays in her native Washington state. "Acting was always what I wanted to do," she told *16*. "At first my parents said, 'Oh, yeah, honey, right,' but when they saw I was serious, they really supported me."

*Free Willy* star Jason James Richter also had something to prove. "I had to wait till my mom would let me—for a six-month period, to make sure it was what I wanted," he told *16*. "Acting is a big commitment." Obviously he proved his point; today, Jason is a bona fide star.

**2.** *Convince Mom and Dad that you won't end up like some former child stars who've appeared on TV talk shows whining about their horrible, messed-up lives.* Naturally your folks don't want you to be unhappy. The best way to overcome their anxieties is to show them the profiles of the young actors in this book.

Sixteen-year-old Paul Sutera (*The Brady Bunch Movie*) agrees. He suggests that you "go out and buy copies of *People* magazine and show your mom and dad articles about kid stars that are really upbeat."

**3.** *Prove to your parents that you really have talent.* Your parents probably won't take your acting career seriously until they're convinced you really have what it takes. The best way to prove you do is to try out for lots of local plays. If you land some major roles, your folks will be forced to sit up and take notice.

If the director of a play or your acting teacher compliments you on your acting ability, ask him to tell your parents. When your folks learn that adults think their little darling is talented, they'll start to pay attention.

Finally, send your photograph and resume to some talent agents (read Chapter Five to find out how). If agents start asking you to come in for interviews, it might impress your parents. If you can talk Mom and Dad into taking you to the interviews and an agent decides she wants to sign you, the agent will try to convince your parents to let you act. That may be what it takes to prove to them you have star quality.

**4.** *Point out to your parents that the money you earn can help pay for your college education.* Tell them about the boy in the Boston Chicken commercial who made thousands of dollars just by sitting there. That kid could be you!

**5.** *Promise your parents you won't play any parts that they don't approve of.* Remind them that even when children are hired to play roles in adult TV shows and movies, the children are sheltered from bad language and violence whenever possible. "They're pretty good about that," Mary Richards says about her daughter's role on *General Hospital.* "In fact, if her TV mom is doing a scene where she doesn't feel comfortable, she'll say, 'I want the children off the set.'"

**6.** *Point out that kids who act in TV series and movies get their schooling from a private teacher on the set.* That's like getting a personal tutor for free. Olivia Hack's mom says, "My husband would like Olivia to do a sitcom because she would have her own private teacher. She'd be in a controlled environment. She wouldn't be in public school around kids with guns and knives."

Tell your parents that being an actor doesn't mean your schoolwork has to suffer. In many states, child actors must maintain at least a C average or their work permits are revoked. "We don't have to fuss about his grades," explains Paul Sutera's mother, "because he has to keep them up to get his work permit."

**7.** *Show your parents these upbeat quotes from the parents of young working actors:*

**Mea Hack:** "There's a chance to travel, and you meet a lot of interesting people, plus you can put some money in the bank for college."

**Janet Gaines:** "If Noah is in a play like *A Chorus Line* or *Cabaret*—if it's a mature subject—then it gives us a chance to talk about those issues. It brings them up, rather than never talking about them."

**Laura Jensen:** "I have a totally different perspective on models now. The models are really gorgeous people and you always imagine they're snotty. But they're some of the nicest people I've ever met."

**Mea Hack:** "If Olivia's working on a national commercial, we get really good food—smoked salmon, cappuccino."

**Cynthia Toovey:** "When we first started out, we were very leery [of show business]. But Shawn's manager handles things well. She's good at what she does."

**Mea Hack:** "It makes kids self-assured. I can send Olivia off to any dinner party and know she can hold her own. She has a lot of self-confidence, and that's going to take her a long way in life."

# Up Close and Personal:

# Jim and Cynthia Toovey

Most people are familiar with the stereotype of the overbearing stage parent—the mother or father who pushes their little darling into show business, hoping to see their child become a star. But not all parents of child stars are like that. Just look at Jim and Cynthia Toovey, whose son Shawn can be seen on the CBS television series *Dr. Quinn, Medicine Woman.*

When Shawn first began modeling for a San Antonio, Texas, department store at age six, his father was a truck driver and his mother was a homemaker. Grooming their son to be a TV star was the last thing on their minds. But all that changed when a Houston talent manager, Lee Peterson, told them their son had star potential.

Jim, a naturally low-key kind of guy, was interested but cautious. Cynthia, too, was hesitant to get her son seriously involved in show business, but she admits she was pretty excited. "It's hard not thinking about

Shawn and his parents relax outside his trailer on the set of *Dr. Quinn, Medicine Woman.*

fame and money when you start—just realizing the possibilities you didn't know were there. In the back of my mind I thought, 'Wow, my son might be famous!'"

Eventually, Jim and Cynthia did decide to sign with Peterson. Little did they know they would soon be faced with their first big show business decision. When Shawn was offered a part in an HBO movie that called for him to use obscene language, it was up to his parents to decide whether he should take the role.

"Oh, my gosh . . . I stayed up all night!" Cynthia exclaims. "This was so new to us and it's hard not to get excited about the prospect of doing a movie. I thought, 'He's never going to get another project.' But at the same time I wanted to come out of this with my dignity. So there were a lot of mixed feelings."

Finally, Jim and Cynthia decided to turn down the role. Shawn's manager stood behind them. "It's a mutual agreement between Lee and me," Cynthia explains. "We don't want Shawn doing anything that's in bad taste."

Soon after they turned down the HBO movie, Shawn snagged a part in another television movie. Cynthia found herself walking onto her very first movie set, meeting stars she had seen on television, and being expected to know her way around. "At first, I just couldn't talk," she recalls. "The first couple of projects I'd be sitting there thinking, 'I'm sitting on a movie set!'"

But it wasn't all bright lights and movie stars. When Shawn wasn't acting in TV movies or commercials, his mother was taking him to auditions. "There were times back in Texas when we'd drive five or six hours to Dallas for an audition and back again.

We'd get home and they'd call the next morning and say, 'We need you for a callback [a follow-up audition].' And we'd turn around and drive back."

At the auditions, Cynthia would help Shawn study his lines, then wait while he went in to try out. "It's nerve-wracking sitting out there thinking, 'What's going on in there?' " she admits. Even in the lobby, the atmosphere was competitive. "You're sitting there and all the mothers are sizing up the other mothers and looking at the other kids," she explains. "That was a little overwhelming at first. But I got used to it. You just tune out."

Fortunately, both Shawn and his parents don't take rejection personally. "There were times when Shawn didn't get a part and I thought, 'Oh, darn, I wanted [him to get] it,' " Cynthia says. "But that feeling passes because the way it works is that you go for an audition and you know it's going to take a few days to hear back. Meanwhile, you go on another audition and another. So they sort of fade, and sometimes you literally forget. It's an ongoing thing."

In 1992, Shawn was selected to play the role of Brian Cooper in the *Dr. Quinn, Medicine Woman* pilot. He and his mother lived in a hotel in Los Angeles while the pilot was being filmed. When the series was picked up by the network, they moved to a furnished apartment. Jim, who had quit his truck driving job and was doing freelance photography, moved out to be with them. "I didn't want to be there [in Texas] alone," he remembers. "It had to be a family thing."

They soon discovered that having a child in a TV series was a full-time job. "We have to be within sound of him the whole time he's on the set," Cynthia explains. "We have to be available to give approval in case they have to make a decision, make sure he gets where he's supposed to be on time—just basically oversee the whole thing."

One thing that didn't change much was their finances. When you have a child in a TV series, Cynthia explains, California law requires that you go before a judge and state ". . . what your expenses are and what you project. Then the judge decides what percentage of the child's salary will be put into a locked account and what percentage you can use for expenses. Nobody can get into the account until the child is eighteen."

Another thing that didn't change was their relationship with their son. "When he leaves the set, he's just Shawn," his father insists. "We made an agreement that acting is just going to be a part of his life. He does other things."

"I don't want Shawn to be a person who demands attention," Cynthia adds. "I want him to get enough from Jim and me that the other people don't matter. It's nice, it's fun, but it isn't essential."

In fact, Jim and Cynthia wouldn't even mind if Shawn decided to quit acting someday. "Whatever he chooses to do later on, that's fine," Cynthia says emphatically.

But for now, Shawn's main focus is acting. And that means it's Jim and Cynthia's focus, too. Luckily, it's something they enjoy. "We expected to meet a lot of nasty people [in show business]," Jim says, "but every project we've been on we've come away with friends."

But how do they feel watching their son get so much attention? Do they ever feel left out? "We're not the ones in the spotlight," Cynthia admits, "but it's not like we aren't doing anything—there are the negotiations, and dealing with his manager about things. I enjoy doing that part."

"It's fun for me to see all this happening to Shawn," Jim agrees. "It's not like I feel subordinate."

With so much experience under their belts, it's only natural that Jim and Cynthia have strong opinions about what it takes to be a good stage parent. "It takes the kind of parents who make their children a priority in their lives," Cynthia says. "It takes that kind of dedication to go all the way in show business. The kids are just out there having fun, but it's the parents who deal with the politics."

"If Shawn wasn't an only child, I don't know how we could do this," Jim adds. "It takes a lot of time."

What does the future hold for Shawn and his parents? "I sort of let things happen," Cynthia says. "I'm not the kind of person who likes to sit down and plan years into the future. I like to just see what feels natural and go with it."

In the final analysis, all that really matters to Jim and Cynthia is that their son be happy. "If something happens and this ends tomorrow, I get to go home with Shawn and spend the rest of my life with him," Cynthia says. "These other people will go on their way and he'll have touched their lives. But I get to be his mother. That's all I want."

# CHAPTER ★ 4

# SMALL-TOWN HEARTTHROBS

**O**kay, you've acted in some amateur plays. You've taken acting lessons. Your parents are ready and willing to help you make it in show biz. What do you do next?

For most people, the answer is: get an agent. Agents help actors find work. When a casting director is looking for children to appear on a commercial, in a movie, or in a newspaper or magazine ad, he calls up a talent agent. Agents also subscribe to "breakdown services" (companies that publicize listings of upcoming

> There's potential work out there for just about everyone—with or without acting experience.
>
> *—William Paul Steele, in his book* Stay Home and Star!

productions and the acting roles that are being cast). The agent looks through her files for kids who seem right for the parts. Then she calls the kids and sends them out on auditions.

Most agents are located in large cities like Los Angeles, New York, Chicago, and Dallas. There are also talent agencies that represent kids in medium-sized cities like Nashville, Phoenix, Boston, and Honolulu. If you live in or near a major city, an agent is the way to go. But what if you live in a small town, a hundred miles from the nearest big city? Can you still rocket to stardom, or are your dreams of success destined to crash and burn?

## Going It Alone

Even if you live out in the boondocks, it *is* possible to land some real acting and modeling jobs. All it takes is desire, hard work, and plenty of nerve. Here are some of the small-town jobs available for young models and actors:

Every small town has businesses that advertise locally. They may run print ads in the local newspaper or produce low-budget commercials that are shown on cable television or broadcast on the radio. Stores and businesses also print up pamphlets and posters advertising and explaining their services. If you live in a popular vacation spot, your local chamber of commerce may produce tourist brochures.

Television and radio stations produce commercials to advertise upcoming local shows. They also make public-service announcements (commercials that advertise nonprofit agencies, like the Red Cross, or events, like the Special Olympics). Also, if your cable company has a cable-access channel, there are probably lots of local people producing low-budget shows for the station.

Department stores often sponsor fashion shows or hire freeze models (models who stand in the store window wearing the latest fashions).

Large and medium-sized companies make industrial films (training films that are shown to their employees, or films that advertise their products to distributors).

All these businesses use local models and actors to appear in their commercials, print ads, fashion shows, and industrials. If you can get in touch with the people who create the ads and run the fashion shows—and you can convince them you have talent—there's a good chance they will hire you. Here's how:

## Say Cheese

Whether you're contacting a local business, an advertising agency, or an agent, the first thing you need is a few photographs of yourself and a resume. Since you're just beginning in show business and you're probably growing and changing rapidly, it doesn't make sense to spend a lot of money to have a professional photograph taken. Two or three clear, well-lighted snapshots (color or black-and-white) that show your face clearly will do.

Don't wear makeup. "I get parents sending me pictures of their three-year-old little girls with so much makeup on," says Wendy Lee. "I'll call them and say, 'I'm sorry, I can't tell what your child looks like. You have to send me a picture without any makeup.'"

Try a few different poses—one dressed up, one in

A good amateur photo is all it takes to launch your local acting career. Here, ten-year-old Claudia Lopez charms the camera.

shorts and a T-shirt, one sitting down, one wearing in-line skates or carrying a skateboard. Make sure the photos are in focus and don't have any shadows blocking your face. Smile and try your best to project energy, personality, and enthusiasm.

Write your name, birth date, address, and phone number on the back of each picture in case they get separated from your resume.

Your resume should give your name, address, phone number, birth date, and age. It should also list your height, weight, eye color, hair color, and clothing size. Next, list all the performances you've been in—school plays, church pageants, dance recitals, everything. Your credentials may not seem impressive to you, but they show you've spent time in front of an audience.

Also list any acting, dancing, singing, or modeling

classes you've taken. Finally, list any special skills you have—anything from speaking with an English accent to playing soccer to knowing how to juggle. Who knows? The fact that you can wiggle your ears and play the flute—two skills that may seem totally uninteresting to you—could be the reason why you land a role while dozens of other talented actors are turned away.

## Is Anybody Out There?

Your next job is to get in touch with the people in your area who create the commercials, print ads, TV shows, and industrials. If the thought of contacting a bunch of adults you don't even know leaves you tongue-tied and quaking in your Nikes, you can ask your parents or some other responsible adult to do it for you. But remember, people in the entertainment industry are impressed by kids who are outgoing, personable, and motivated. If you can find the nerve to pick up the phone yourself, people will remember you. And in the world of show biz, that's exactly what you want.

The first part is easy. All you have to do is watch television for a few days and check out the local commercials. You'll be able to recognize them: the commercials will mention the addresses of businesses that you know are in your town, and the commercials will be very simple and straightforward, using no famous actors and few special effects. Also, look through the newspaper for any local print ads that use models.

Of course, not all businesses produce print ads and commercials that feature young people. For example, a local bar is definitely not going to hire you to be in their commercial. But you'd be surprised how many businesses try to appeal to families—restaurants, banks, clothing stores, pet shops, barber shops, even car dealerships. And if a business caters to families, that means their commercials will probably include kids.

Once you've checked out the local ads, look up each business in the phone book to get its address and phone number. Now you're ready to start networking.

## *Phone Tag*

Call up each business and ask to speak with the director of advertising. Be patient. If you can't get through to the ad director the first time you call, ask her secretary when it would be convenient to call back. Keep trying until you get her.

When you get the director of advertising on the phone, ask whether the company makes its own commercials or uses an advertising agency. If the company makes its own commercials, tell her that you are a young actor looking for work and ask if you can send her your photo and resume. If she agrees, send them. Then call back two weeks later to make sure she received them and to ask if you can come in and meet her.

If she says she can't meet with you, don't consider it a rejection. Just remind her you'd love to audition for her, and ask her to keep you in mind for her company's next commercial or print ad. Check back in a month to remind her you're still interested.

If the director of advertising agrees to meet you in person, dress neatly but casually. Act natural and let her see you're relaxed, outgoing, and enthusiastic.

She'll probably ask you how you got interested in acting. Be upbeat and cheerful. Don't pressure her to hire you. Just be friendly and let her know you're always ready to come in for an audition. After the "interview" is over, go home and write her a thank-you letter. Tell her you enjoyed the meeting and you hope to hear from her soon.

If the company uses an advertising agency to produce its commercials, ask the director of advertising for the name of the agency and the name of the account executive who handles the company's account. Call the advertising agency and ask to speak to the account executive. Say basically all the same things you would have said to the director of advertising—you're a young actor, you want to audition for acting jobs, you'd like to send him your photo and resume, and so on.

Television stations and radio stations also produce commercials. You can look up your local stations in the Yellow Pages. Call and ask for the person in charge of producing commercials—his title will probably be production manager or production director. Again, tell him you're a young actor looking for work and ask if you can send your photo and resume. Radio stations will probably also want an audio demonstration tape (a cassette tape that shows off your voice). Find some print advertisements in family magazines and record yourself reading two or three different ads. Ads for kids' products work well. Keep your demo tape short— no longer than three minutes.

If there are some medium-sized or large companies in your area—a hospital or health care organization, a manufacturing plant, a computer software company—

they may produce in-house industrial films. The films might be employee training videos, videos about new company policies and procedures, or videos promoting the company's products for distributors. Call the companies and ask who is in charge of producing their industrials. If they are produced in-house, speak to the person in charge and ask if you can send your photo and resume. Be sure to mention your age—not all industrials use young actors.

In some areas of the country, there are also independent production houses that produce commercials and industrials. Look in the Yellow Pages under the headings *television production, video production services,* or *audio production.* Call each production house and ask to speak to a producer. Once again, tell him who you are and ask if you can send your photo and resume.

Finally, call the local department stores and ask if they ever organize fashion shows. Speak to the person in charge and ask where she finds her models. Tell her you are eager to model, and ask if you can send your photograph. As always, try to set up a personal interview. A photograph can be tossed aside; a phone call can be ignored. But if you're face to face with the person in power, she will be forced to deal with you directly. If you make a good impression and show her you're eager but not pushy, she'll remember you when a modeling or acting job comes along.

### When the Big Boys Come to Town

Sometimes national companies—like Sears, Burger King, or Exxon—will produce regional commercials. The cost is lower, and they can take advantage of the local scenery. Television shows and movies are often filmed on location, too. For example, the movie *Man-2-Man,* starring Jonathan Taylor Thomas, was shot in Vancouver, British Columbia, Canada, and the TV series *seaQuest DSV* is filmed in Florida.

Large department stores and mail-order catalogs also photograph models on location. For example, European clothing companies come to Arizona in the winter to shoot their summer swimsuit catalogs. Why? "Seven months of the year we have good weather," explains agent Monika Simmons.

When a national or international company arrives in a small town to shoot a commercial, the casting director often hires local actors for the smaller roles. Television and movie companies also hire local performers for small roles and as extras (nonspeaking parts). Catalogs use local models, too.

Most models and actors are hired through talent agencies, but it is possible to land a job on your own. The best way to find out about film crews and photographers who are shooting in your area is to read your local newspaper. If a movie or commercial is being filmed in your town—especially if a famous actor is involved—there will be an article about it. Call the newspaper and speak to the reporter who wrote the article. Ask him where the production crew is staying and try to get a name or two. Then call the production office, tell them who you are, and ask if they're auditioning local actors.

When casting directors need extras for a TV show, movie, or regional commercial, they often put ads in the local paper. Extra work doesn't pay well, but it will give you a chance to get behind the scenes and learn how a real movie is shot. Plus, there's always the chance you can make some contacts while you're hanging around the set.

## Networking for Fun and Profit

One of the best ways to get jobs in a small town is by getting to know people. Ask around. Do any of your friends' parents work for businesses that advertise on TV or in the newspaper? Maybe they can get you an interview with the company's director of advertising.

Do you know anyone who works for the local TV station, radio station, or newspaper? Ask if they can set up a tour of the station or the news office for you. While you're there, introduce yourself to everyone and tell them you're a young actor eager to land some work.

Is there a community college in your area? If the school offers film and video classes, you might be able to land a job acting in a student film. Call the school and ask to speak to the film teacher. Put up a notice on the school bulletin board advertising your talents.

Do you take acting or dancing lessons? Talk to your teacher. She probably knows some of the local performers and producers. Tell her you're itching to perform in front of a camera and ask her if she can introduce you to some of the local talent.

## Small-Town Stars

Once you make contact with the people who produce commercials, print ads, and local TV and radio shows in your area, the next step is to wait for someone to invite you to an audition. An audition is

Noah Gaines has acted in dozens of plays in his hometown.

your chance to show the people in power what you can do. If they like what they see, they'll offer you a job. (For more information on auditioning, see Chapter Six: Strutting Your Stuff.)

Small-town jobs don't pay much—in fact, you may be asked to work for free when you're first starting out—but at least you'll be getting experience and making contacts. And remember, one job leads to another. Once your name and face become known around town, advertisers will start calling *you*.

Twelve-year-old Noah Gaines rarely has to search for local acting work anymore. "The more you work, the more you get around, the more people know about you and tell their friends," he explains. "That's how you get jobs."

# CHAPTER 5

# WHEN AN AGENT IS THE ANSWER

If small-town stardom isn't enough to satisfy you, the next step is to start looking for work in the nearest major metropolitan area. In order to land modeling and acting jobs in the big city, you'll probably need an agent. But how do you find one?

I go through 100 pictures a week and try to figure out which kids I should bring in for an interview.

—*Denver, Colorado, talent agent Wendy Lee*

## Come and Get Me

One way is to let the agents come to you. If you live near a big city and you perform in plays, one night you may discover that there's an agent in the audience searching for new talent. "I go out to plays a lot," says

Arizona agent Monika Simmons. "I did that in L.A., and I do it here."

Noah Gaines lives in Santa Barbara, California. He was performing in a play called *Flavia and the Dream Maker* when he was spotted by a visiting agent from Los Angeles. After the show, she invited him to L.A. for an interview and eventually signed him.

Another way to let the agents discover you is to attend an acting workshop or seminar run by professionals. The National Association of Showbiz Kids, for example, is a nonprofit organization based in New Jersey that teaches young wannabes about the business. For a $35 fee, they will set up a screen test for you in front of show biz professionals. If the pros are impressed, Showbiz Kids will advise you on the basics of finding an agent. For another $47 they will mail your photo and resume to one hundred New York talent agencies.

Another way to make the agents notice you is to enter a national modeling or talent contest. Lacey Chabert was a junior vocalist finalist on *Star Search* before she landed the role of Claudia on the TV series *Party of Five*. Matt Jensen of Phoenix, Arizona, was ten years old when he heard an ad on the radio for a talent contest called the National Showcase Awards (now out of business). The acting category was full, so he entered in the modeling category and was chosen "most photogenic male." One of the judges was Robert Black, owner of the Robert Black Agency in Tempe, Arizona. Matt is now signed with his agency.

Keep your eyes open for big talent contests. They will be advertised on TV and radio or in magazines and newspapers. But don't let yourself get ripped off.

Find out who the contest judges are. If they aren't working show biz professionals—such as agents, casting directors, producers—then they can't help your career.

Sometimes major motion pictures and TV shows (especially reality-based shows like *Rescue 911*) are shot on location. If a movie or TV show is being filmed in your area, the casting director may advertise an open audition. Listen to Chris Demetral, star of the HBO show *Dream On* and the movie *Blank Check*: ". . . when I was eleven, my grandmother found an ad for an open audition—for *Night of the Living Dead II*. I didn't get the part, but the casting director helped me find an agent. I've been working ever since."

And, of course, there's always the million-to-one chance that an agent will be hanging around the mall or the corner minimart, scouting for new talent. "I was in line for a ride at a school festival," Mike Vitar, star of *The Mighty Ducks* told *16,* "and this guy came over and gave me his card. He said he was a professional manager and asked if I wanted to be in show business." Mike said yes, and the rest is history.

## Go Get 'Em

If the agents won't come to you, you'll have to go to them. Your first job is to find out the names and addresses of the talent agencies that operate in your area. For starters, check out the Yellow Pages of the phone book. You can also write to the Screen Actors Guild (5757 Wilshire Boulevard, Los Angeles, CA 90036) to get a list of SAG-franchised agents throughout the country. Enclose three dollars and a self-addressed, stamped envelope.

It's easy to get a list of agents, but how do you know which ones are hard-working and successful? One way to find out is to contact the art directors or producers at your local advertising agencies. Ask them which agents they call when they need models and actors.

You can also talk to other actors in your area and find out who represents them. Ask them if they're happy with their agent. If an actor says yes—and you know him fairly well—ask him if he'll recommend you to his agent. An agent is more likely to take a serious look at you if you're referred by one of his or her clients.

Sometimes acting, dance, and gymnastics teachers are friendly with local agents. Ask your teacher for a recommendation. Some schools even hold showcases where kids can strut their stuff for local agents.

Do you know anyone who is in any way connected with show business? Any connection, no matter how distant, can help. When Kellie Martin (*Life Goes On, Christy*) was seven years old, her aunt was a nanny for Michael Landon's children. Auntie wrangled Kellie an audition, which led to a guest spot on the TV show *Father Murphy*—and an agent.

If you can't get a recommendation, you'll have to contact the agents in your area by yourself. That's fine—many aspiring young actors have found agents that way. Here's what to do:

First, call the agency and make sure they represent children and teenagers. Not all agencies do. Next, be sure you have their correct address. Ask for the name of the agent who handles children, and make sure you write down the correct spelling.

Write a brief letter to each agent explaining that

you are a young actor seeking representation. Send along two or three terrific snapshots and your resume.

It normally takes four to six weeks to get a reply from an agent, so be patient. If you don't hear from him, it probably means he isn't interested. But it doesn't hurt to make a follow-up call.

Try phoning in the late afternoon. Agents are busy in the morning reading the "breakdowns" and sending their clients on auditions. If you do get the agent on the phone, ask him if he received your photos and if he's interested in you. Be friendly and eager, but not pushy.

Sometimes a follow-up phone call can make all the difference. Just ask Matt Jensen. After winning a modeling contest, he sent his photo to the Robert Black Agency in Tempe, Arizona, but didn't receive a reply. "Matt started bothering me to call," his mother remembers. "I was too embarrassed, so I said, 'If you're interested, you call.' So he did—he's very bold." Agent Kimberly Johnson was so impressed with his poise and enthusiasm that she invited him in for an interview—and eventually signed him.

### Face-to-Face

If an agent likes your photos and resume, he'll ask you and your parent or guardian to come in for an interview. How does the agent decide who to interview? Listen to Lucy Silver, a former New York agent, and now a manager: "For every thirty pictures, I called in about six of the children to my office for an interview, or to do a monologue, or to try a cold reading," she says in *The Young Performer's Guide.* "Certainly an actor's experiences or credits had something to do with it, but most kids simply don't have major credits. I'd say it was something behind the eyes in the photo that just told me that this might be an interesting person and it would be worth my while to get to know him or her."

If an agent calls you in for an interview, don't panic! Dress casually and don't wear makeup. Show up on time. The agent will chat with you and your parent. He'll ask your age, what you do for fun, why you want to act, and lots of other questions. Don't freeze up, don't try to perform, and definitely don't act coy or cutesy. Just be yourself.

"I can tell in one second if the child has it or not," says casting director Nancy Smith. "Any kid who comes in, makes eye contact, and says, 'Hi. How are you?' is usually going to be okay. If a kid comes in and grabs his mother's leg and hides behind it, or if he comes in with his head down, walking slow—that kid I wouldn't touch with a ten-foot pole."

"I looked for the child who had interest!" Lucy Silver says in *The Young Performer's Guide*. "I looked for the child who was well adjusted, who did well in school. . . . I looked for a child who was inquisitive and who asked a lot of questions."

Agents like kids who are confident and know what they want. Listen to Wendy Lee: "I had a ten-year-old boy walk into my office the other day and look me in the eye and say, 'Hi. I'd like to introduce myself. My name is Wayne Wallace, and I'd like to do some modeling.' And I thought, 'This is a great kid. He knows what he wants.'"

Nancy Smith agrees. "I had a little red-headed boy come over the other day," she says. "He shook my hand

and went right for my dog and started petting him. He talked a mile a minute. I knew this kid was great. I sent him out [for a job] the next day."

Remember, your parents are being interviewed, too. "I looked for children whose parents were supportive of their lives and their extracurricular activities," says Lucy Silver. "The parents shouldn't be pushy."

"From the parent I look for someone who is not living their fantasies through their child," explains Monika Simmons. "The parents have to be financially stable and emotionally stable."

### Sign on the Dotted Line

If an agent is sufficiently impressed with your talent and charisma, *and* he thinks you and your parent or guardian are serious about pursuing an acting career, he will offer to represent you. In most cases that will mean he wants you to sign a contract giving him the exclusive right to represent you for a year or more. In some cases, an agent may suggest a verbal contract—nothing in writing, just a spoken agreement that can be ended whenever either of you wants out.

Now the ball is in your court. But wait. Don't sign anything on the spot. Sure, it's thrilling to think that a real honest-to-goodness agent wants to represent you. In fact, if you're a brand new actor, you're probably thinking this is your one and only shot at stardom. If you don't sign on the dotted line right this minute, you'll never get another chance.

Wrong. If one agent wants to sign you, the odds are good that others will, too. Besides, it's better to have no agent at all than to have a bad one. So before you do anything, you and your stage parent should ask yourself some important questions: Is this guy legit, or is he trying to take me for a ride? Will he work hard for me? Do I trust him? Here's how to find out.

## The Sleaze Factor

First of all, you need to ask the agent what kind of auditions he will send you on. Some agencies only represent models; some will only send you out for commercial auditions. Other agencies also handle TV and film work. If you sign with a models-only agency, it's okay to find another agent to represent you for acting work. Be sure to talk this over with your agent before you sign the contract.

Next, you need to know that the agent is reputable and honest. Is the agency franchised by the Screen Actors Guild or by the American Federation of Television and Radio Artists? That's a plus, because SAG- and AFTRA-franchised agents must follow certain rules and guidelines. If the agency is not franchised by SAG or AFTRA, check out the contract carefully. If possible, have an entertainment lawyer review it before you sign it.

You should be wary of agents who advertise for models and actors in the newspapers. Legitimate agents get dozens of phone calls every day from actors who want to be represented by their agency. They don't need to advertise.

A red flag should go up if the agent says you must get professional photos taken by the photographer of her choice. Agents who say that are usually getting a kickback from the photographer for every client they send over. It's okay for the agent to suggest some photographers, but she shouldn't pressure you.

Also beware of agents who promise you the moon. If he swears you're going to be bigger than Macaulay Culkin and promises to get you a guest shot on *Roseanne* by the end of the year, start running. You can't trust him.

Most important, never sign with an agent who wants you to pay him money up front. Legitimate agents don't make money until you do. Then they earn a commission—usually 10 percent of your earnings. Agent Wendy Lee tells of a modeling agency in Denver that charges a fee just to look at a child's photo. "They'll accept pretty much anyone, but they only send out a small number of kids to auditions," she warns. "They have maybe five hundred clients, but probably only fifty of them are working."

You must decide if the agent is going to work hard for you. How many clients does he represent? Can you talk to a few of them? If he says no, that's not a good sign. If he says yes, call them up. Ask what kind of jobs the agent has gotten them and if they've been happy with their contracts. Also, get a feeling for what kind of kids the agency handles.

As casting director Judy Belshe explains, "Every agency has a personality because the person who owns it trains their agents to pick a certain look and type. When I was with the Kalman/Arletta Agency, for example, we picked kids who were lovable. They could be quirky-looking or funny-looking, but they were downright lovable. You wanted to look at them again."

Does the agency that wants to sign you specialize in your look and type? If so, that's a plus.

Finally, you need to trust your instincts. Do you feel comfortable talking to the agent? Does she look you in the eye? Does she seem real? If you like her style and you think you can work with her—*and* she's honest and ethical—then get out your pen and start signing.

## What More Do I Need?

Some young actors have a manager as well as an agent. Some have a manager *instead* of an agent. So what exactly is a manager, and why would you want one?

Talent agents usually represent a large number of actors—anywhere from fifty to over two hundred. With a client list that big, your agent can't give you much personal attention. The most you can expect from her is to be sent on lots of auditions, and to be able to rely on her to negotiate good contracts.

A manager, on the other hand, oversees the actor's entire career. He works with a small number of clients and gives each of them personal attention. He helps them decide which roles they should audition for, and which they should take. He works with them to develop their look and image. He recommends acting teachers, photographers, and publicists. He also makes contacts that can further the actor's career.

Richard Glasser is the owner of Double R Management, a full-service Hollywood management company that represents several young stars. "We go to the studios," he says. "We take producers out to lunch, we get scripts, we create jobs for the client."

A good manager will prevent you from wasting your time on useless auditions. "I considered getting a manager for Robyn just before she started *General Hospital*," explains her mother, Mary Richards, "because I was so tired of driving to L.A. for inappropriate auditions. A manager can weed out what's appropriate and what's not, but an agent doesn't have time."

Technically, managers cannot book jobs for their clients unless they also are licensed as agents. "But what happens is that through their contacts, they drum up business," explains Richard Glasser. "Then the agent negotiates."

Some young actors are managed by their parents. If your stage parent has a head for business and is ready to undertake a new, demanding career, the arrangement can work. One young actor who is managed by her mother told *Callback* magazine, "It brings me closer to her in two ways because she's involved in my personal life and professional life. That makes it extra special."

But being managed by your mom or dad can cause problems. Listen to manager and casting director Breanna Benjamin: "It's my opinion that the child needs the emotional support from the parent as the parent," she writes in *The Young Performer's Guide*. "The parent should be the child's shoulder to cry on, the reward at the end of the hard day's work, not the one who says, 'You should have done this.'"

If you're acting just for the fun of it, or if you're only trying to land commercial and print work, you probably don't need a manager. But if you dream of a lifelong career in show business, a manager may be the answer. So how do you find one?

Exactly the same way you find an agent—through

your fellow actors' recommendations, by performing somewhere a manager will see you, or by contacting managers yourself. The tricky part is knowing whom to trust. Unlike agents, managers aren't licensed or regulated in any way. And they can charge whatever commission they choose—usually 20 percent and up.

The best way to judge if a manager is legit is to find out if he belongs to the NCOPM, the National Conference of Personal Managers (210 East 51st Street, New York, NY 10022), an organization that develops ethical guidelines for personal managers. You can also ask the manager which agents he works with. Successful managers associate themselves with successful agents. Finally, just as you did when choosing an agent, you need to ask questions and talk to some of the manager's clients. Then go with your instincts.

"It's networking," says Joyce Sutera when asked why her son Paul has an agent *and* a manager. "Everybody knows different people. I think the more contacts you have and the bigger your support team, the better it is. It's a team effort."

## Shoot Me Again

Congratulations! You have an agent or a manager and you're ready to land some jobs. Well—not quite. Before your agent can send you out on auditions, he needs professional photographs of you to submit to casting agents. And guess what? Supplying the photos is your responsibility, not his.

Before the camera can begin clicking, you must decide what kind of photos you need. Talk to your agent or manager to get his point of view. If you plan to audition mainly for print work and commercial

A composite card is a must for print and commercial work. Here, Matt Jensen shows off two different looks.

jobs, you'll need a composite card (a series of black-and-white shots, showing yourself in various poses—for example, dressed up, in casual clothes, playing sports, maybe licking an ice-cream cone). If it's noncommercial film and theatrical jobs you're hoping for, a headshot (a single black-and-white, 8" by 10" portrait of your face) is best.

In both cases, your photo should display tons of energy and personality that almost jumps off the page. In the video *Modeling, Commercials & Acting,* model Denise Richards gives this advice: "Your photograph should concentrate on capturing a genuine look and the essence of who you are. For commercial headshots, a big smile is what they want. For theatrical and film work, they want a real sincere you. In both cases, good eye contact is a must."

How will you find the photographer who will help

you create this amazing photograph? Your agent or manager will probably have some recommendations. You should also talk to your fellow actors, check out their headshots, and ask which photographers they used.

Once you have the names of a few photographers, it's up to you to select the one you like. "One of the hardest decisions you'll have to make is determining if the photographer you're about to choose is a fly-by-night," professional photographer Dianora Niccolini warns in *The Young Performer's Guide.* "The two best ways of assessing the situation are by actually visiting the studio to look at the photographer's portfolio and to get a price list or *prices in writing.*"

Whatever you do, don't hire a photographer who isn't experienced in show biz photography. You won't end up with a top-notch photograph—and as a result, casting directors who see your photo won't take you seriously.

At the photo session, bring three or four changes of clothing. Pastel colors photograph best; don't wear black or white. Don't wear anything that's distracting (like clunky jewelry) or too trendy (like a T-shirt with the name of your favorite rock band printed across the front). Most of all, be yourself. Stay relaxed and have fun posing for the camera. You want your final photograph to look exactly like you do on your very best day.

After your photographer develops the photos, he will give you a "proof sheet" or "contact sheet" (a page containing small copies of the photos he took). Make sure he also gives you the negatives. It's up to you to pick the best photos and get them printed. Don't decide by yourself. Show the photos to your agent, manager, acting teacher, fellow actors—anyone who knows something about show business.

Top-quality professional photos can cost big bucks—a hundred dollars and up for the photo session and another two hundred to three hundred dollars for the reproductions. If your family absolutely can't come up with the money, talk to your agent or manager. Maybe he can find you a deal.

Remember, your headshot is your business card. Casting directors and producers will see it before they see you. Be sure your photos make them sit up and say, "Wow! I've just got to meet this kid!"

# Up Close and Personal:
# Olivia Hack

Talk about starting young! Olivia Hack starred in her first commercial when she was just eight months old. Since then, the busy twelve-year-old has been in over thirty commercials, four TV shows, three plays, and two feature films. But it hasn't all been a piece of cake. When you ask Olivia how many auditions she's done that *didn't* lead to a job, she bursts out laughing. "Don't ask!" she exclaims. "Dozens! *Millions!*"

From the beginning, Olivia, an only child, had show business in her blood—her mother is an actress and playwright; her father is an animation director. But it wasn't her parents' show biz connections that got Olivia her first job. It was her cute face and outgoing personality.

"Olivia was one of those babies you could just hand to someone and she would have a good time," her mother, Mea, remembers. "She was never frightened. She loved being held, and she was very social. Plus,

Olivia Hack

her father always had a camera in her face, and she enjoyed it."

Friends and co-workers told Mea she should get her daughter an agent. "We sent out snapshots to five agents and heard from all five of them," she says. Soon Olivia had her first job—being photographed for an ad in the *Los Angeles Times*. But it soon became apparent that modeling wasn't her cup of tea.

"It was a disaster!" her mother recalls. "She had to wear a sweater, and it was incredibly hot and she had to sit still. There was no interacting with other characters. She hated it!"

Olivia's next job, a Minolta commercial, went much more smoothly. Soon she was working regularly. The first commercial she remembers was for Socrates, a children's computer game. She had to sit on a bed and sing the same song over and over while the crew filmed dozens of takes. Despite the hard work, Olivia had a great time. "It was fun," she insists. "I liked it because I was in a total frilly girl room. It was a fantasy."

When Olivia was four, her family moved from Los Angeles to Toronto, Ontario, Canada. Since Olivia was just starting school, her parents decided she didn't need the distraction of an acting career. When they returned to Los Angeles two years later, she began working again. Almost immediately, it became clear that Olivia had very definite ideas about what kind of acting she wanted to do.

Aside from print work, which she still found boring, she decided she didn't like acting in plays. "It's too much work," she confides. "It's too intense. You do the same thing over and over and over, but you never get to see yourself." On the other hand, TV and film work has always delighted her. She enjoys the idea of having a concrete finished product—a movie or videotape she can keep and view whenever she wants. "They [movies] are around forever," she explains. "Even when the movie is out of the theaters, you can see yourself in video stores and on TV."

But getting those TV and movie roles isn't easy. Not long ago Olivia was up for the lead in the short-lived ABC series *Phenom.* The producers auditioned over two hundred and fifty girls from all over the country before narrowing it down to Olivia and one other actress. "I had twelve callbacks," she remembers with a sigh.

Both girls were invited to the network offices to read a scene with the star of the series, Judith Light. When they finished, a decision was made right on the spot. "One girl got to go straight into rehearsals," Olivia's mother says. "The other got to go home. Olivia was the one who went home."

Another disappointment came when she was up for the lead role in the feature film version of *Heidi.* After numerous callbacks, Olivia was one of the three finalists. In the end, the part went to someone else.

Still, Olivia doesn't let it get her down. "Commercials are not a big, huge deal because there are so many," she says. "If it's TV or movies and it's between me and one or two other girls, then it's a bummer." She shrugs. "But it's like, oh well, I'll get the next one. I keep moving on."

Besides, she insists, dealing with rejection is just part of the business. "After you've lived through it, you can handle just about anything," she says.

With an attitude like that, it will come as no

surprise to learn that auditions rarely make Olivia nervous. One exception was the audition for the role of the little female lion in *The Lion King*. The final audition took place in the studio where they were filming the movie. Olivia and her mother arrived early and found themselves alone in the lobby.

"So we started looking around," her mother remembers. "We looked into a room and there were the original clay models of the characters from *Beauty and the Beast*. And we were overwhelmed . . . we realized she [was auditioning for] the ultimate voice-over prize—to do a voice on a Disney movie." Olivia was so awestruck that she came down with a bad case of nerves. As a result, she blew the audition and didn't get the part.

But there are plenty of jobs Olivia has gotten, including a series of national McDonald's commercials, a featured role in *Star Trek: Generations,* and the part of Cindy, the youngest daughter, in *The Brady Bunch Movie.*

Olivia says the hardest part about filming *The Brady Bunch Movie* was sitting still for an hour every day while the hairdressers put on her wig. And shooting the outdoor scenes in a hot wig in the middle of a Los Angeles heat wave was no picnic either. But there were lots of fun times, too.

"Once we [the Brady kids] were driving down a main street shooting a scene," she recalls with a smile. "Mom and Dad Brady were in the front seat. They were saying their lines and they goofed, but they tried to keep on going. But we just thought, forget it, and we went nuts. We were dancing, the kids playing Greg and Marcia were having a love scene in the backseat—and the actors in the front didn't even realize!"

Olivia has had three different agents during her action-packed career. Her first agency went out of business, and the franchise was bought by another agent. Unfortunately, the new agent didn't always do her job well. "She didn't see Olivia's potential," her mother says. "She was sending her out for the wrong things."

For example, there was the time Olivia got three callbacks for a movie role. At the third audition, the mother of another young actor leaned over to Mea and said, "What do you think of the script? I'm a little concerned about the scene where the girl witnesses the murder."

Olivia's mother was stunned! She had never been told there was a murder scene in the movie. She rushed to the phone and called the agent, who hemmed and hawed. "I don't think she'd read the script," Mea explains. Today Olivia is signed to a top Hollywood agent who represents a number of successful young actors, and those inappropriate auditions are a thing of the past.

What does the future hold for Olivia? For now, she's taking it easy—going to the mall with her friends, playing with her new pet rabbit, enjoying her first year of junior high school, and going on occasional auditions for TV shows and feature films.

But even when Olivia is leading the life of a regular kid, dreams of superstardom are never far from her mind. Someday she hopes to star in a blockbuster movie. "To know I was in it, I was part of what made it earn ninety million!" she exclaims eagerly. "Now *that* would be cool!"

# CHAPTER  6

# STRUTTING YOUR STUFF

**O**nce you've found an agent or manager, or (if you live in a small town) you've made some local contacts, the day will come when you'll be asked to audition for an acting or modeling job. An audition is your chance to convince the casting director, the ad executive, or the producer that you're the perfect person—in fact, the *only* person—for the part. How do you do it? By being prepared, staying calm, and letting your talent and charisma shine.

I wasn't afraid to talk to people. I wasn't afraid to just go for it.

—*Mario Lopez, talking about auditioning for* AKA Pablo, *in the video* Modeling, Commercials & Acting

★   ★   ★

## *Audition for What?*

What kind of jobs will you be auditioning for? If you live in or around a major city like Los Angeles or New York, it could be just about anything. Models are needed for newspaper and magazine print ads, clothing and toy catalogs, and live fashion shows. Actors are needed for plays and musicals, for TV commercials, for guest spots on established TV shows, and for TV pilots (a sample show that may or may not be chosen by networks and syndication companies to be one of their regular series). Actors are also needed for movies—both feature films and industrials—and for voice-over work (recording voices for animated films and TV shows and for radio ads).

If you live in or around a smaller city, you probably won't get many chances to audition for national TV shows or feature films. But that doesn't mean there aren't plenty of jobs available. "Our kids audition for local department store ads, local and regional commercials, for catalogs from Europe and department stores from back East," says Kimberly Johnson from the Robert Black Agency in Tempe, Arizona.

"We get cable shows, a lot of industrials for companies, some feature movies—they come in and cast for the smaller roles," says Wendy Lee of the Donna Baldwin Talent Agency in Denver, Colorado. "We've done a few Movies of the Week. Plus, there's always extra work to be done."

Even if your goal is to be an actor, it's okay to audition for modeling jobs. In fact, it may be the only work available in many small cities. Twelve-year-old Matt Jensen dreams of being a movie star, like his idol, Robin Williams. But for now, he's doing mostly modeling work in Phoenix, Arizona. "He does catalogs for department stores," his mother says. "Adidas has hired him several times. And he did a photo for *Women's World* magazine."

Will you get a chance to audition for every job that exists? No way. If your agent doesn't think you're right for a particular job (for example, if you're the wrong age, wrong sex, or have the wrong look), she won't submit your photograph. And even if your agent does submit your photo, the casting director or producer may not decide to invite you to audition.

But don't fret. Eventually, you *will* get a phone call asking you to come in for an audition. If you have an agent, she will call you and tell you all the important information—what kind of job you're trying out for, when and where to show up, and what to bring (you may be expected to wear a certain type of clothing or to bring sunglasses, a baseball cap, and so on). If you don't have an agent, the ad executive or producer will call you directly.

Be sure to write down all the information, and don't be afraid to ask questions. It's important to be prepared.

### Count Down to Success

Don't stay up late the night before an audition. You want to show up feeling well-rested and energetic. On the day of the audition, eat moderate, well-balanced meals. Avoid sugar—food loaded with sugar can give you dark circles under your eyes.

Make sure your hair is washed and combed and that your fingernails are clean. Don't wear makeup. Wear casual, clean clothing, unless instructed otherwise.

Remember, it was your headshot that got you the audition in the first place. Therefore, you want to show up looking pretty much the way you do in that photograph.

Ask your stage parent to bring along a bag containing things you might need—water, a small snack, a comb or brush, Wet Wipes, Band-Aids, aspirin, a book to read in case you have a long wait. Your stage parent should also bring a datebook in which she can note what you wore to the audition (it's good to wear the same outfit to callbacks) and how many miles you drove (for tax purposes).

Most of all, stay calm. Don't try to anticipate what's going to happen at the audition. What impresses a casting director most in children is not acting technique but naturalness, charm, and honesty. ". . . young actors need to retain their freshness and exuberance," stresses acting teacher Rita Litton in *The Young Performer's Guide.* So just be yourself. And above all, have fun with it.

"When I was a little kid, I'd be so scared," says twelve-year-old Noah Gaines. "My mom would practically have to drag me in there. Then I'd sing and the people would say, 'Good job, Noah,' and I'd think, 'Hey, that wasn't so bad.'"

Matt Jensen had a similar experience. "I was very nervous at my first audition," he says. "I didn't know what to do, really. But I went in there and got it over with, and afterward I thought, 'Whoa, that was a piece of cake!' And after that I wasn't scared anymore."

For ten-year-old Kevin Moody, auditioning is easy. "I just pretend I am doing it in front of my mom and dad," he says in *Kids on Camera.* Try it. It works!

★　★　★

## Getting Off on the Right Foot

Auditions can be held almost anywhere. If you're auditioning for a commercial, movie, or TV pilot, you'll probably be in a casting director's office. Auditions for guest shots on TV shows are usually held in a producer's office on a movie or TV lot. If you're trying out for voice-over work, you'll go to a recording studio. Auditions for plays and musicals are usually in theaters. For print work, most auditions are held in the photographer's studio.

But it's best to be prepared for anything. Mea Hack remembers the time Olivia auditioned for a TV cartoon pilot. "We ended up on this mountain road way out in the [San Fernando] Valley," she says. "It was in this man's home. He had turned one of the rooms into a recording studio. I was concerned, but it turned out to be a legitimate audition."

It's important to be on time, so leave your house early and give yourself plenty of time to get to the audition and find a parking space. Take a map, and don't be afraid to ask directions if you get lost.

The quickest way to make a casting director mad is to show up with all your friends and relatives in tow. Remember, most casting offices are small, and the waiting area will probably be crowded. "Some parents show up with babies and coloring books and diaper bags and food, and the babies are slobbering Skittles on the wall," complains Los Angeles casting director Judy Belshe. "It's too crowded, and it makes our neighbors unhappy. There's a rule in this town: one parent, one child."

If your stage parent finds it necessary to bring along your siblings, try to bring a baby-sitter to care for them. And ask the baby-sitter and your siblings to wait outside.

When you enter the reception area of the office or studio, sign in, using a pen. If there's more than one sign-in sheet, sign them both. Normally, a receptionist or assistant casting director will be there to greet you and give you the sides. Smile and make eye contact. It's important to be friendly and polite to everybody.

Next, sit down and read the sides. Practice your lines, either alone or with your stage parent. Try to ignore the other kids, who will be practicing their lines around you. You don't want to be influenced by what they're doing. Besides, it's a waste of time to worry about the competition. Stay focused and do your own thing.

After you've gone over your lines a few times, stop. You don't want to over-rehearse. The idea is to keep your performance natural and spontaneous.

Finally, don't wait until the last second to comb your hair and straighten your clothes. When you hear your name called, you should be ready to walk in there and knock 'em dead.

## Zero Hour

This is it—the moment you've been waiting for. You're about to do your very first audition. What will it be like?

Picture this: An assistant casting director calls out your name. You say good-bye to your stage parent and follow the assistant down a hallway. She opens a door, and you walk into a room. Sitting behind a desk are two or three adults. One of them shuffles some papers, clears her throat, and says, "Good afternoon."

This is your moment to shine, so give it all you've got. "It's very important to make a good first impression," advises talent agent Wendy Lee. "You want to be able to introduce yourself, smile, shake a hand if it's offered. Be real nice and personable."

Remember, these people have probably spent the entire day auditioning kid after kid after kid. It's up to you to make them remember you. So stand up straight, look them in the eye, and speak up. Even if your knees are knocking under your jeans, you want to appear as though you're absolutely glowing with self-confidence.

Okay, you've gotten the introductions out of the way. Now what?

### Print Jobs

For print work, auditions are fairly simple. The photographer and art director will probably chat with you and look through your portfolio (a photo album containing your previous work), if you have one. Often, the photographer will take some snapshots of you. When the camera starts to click, your job is to show everyone you've got lots of energy and personality.

This is how Ed Ims, director of Showbiz Kids, puts it: "You want a child who has lots of facial expression and great body language. You want motion; you want the person to look alive and moving. You don't want a kid who stands there like a fire plug."

### Commercials

For commercial auditions, you may be asked to read your lines, either with a casting director or with another child actor. Or you may be asked to improvise.

"Sometimes they'll have you do crazy stuff," says Shawn Toovey. "One time I had to run around the room and fly a kite."

"We'll give a child a circumstance," says Ed Ims, "like you just came home and all the lights were out in your house, and all of a sudden fifteen of your friends jump out and yell, 'Surprise! Happy birthday!' What kind of expression can you give us, using both hands and face?"

The idea is to be enthusiastic without appearing fake. "Kids have to get a lot of energy up," says Judy Belshe. "You have to convey some kind of message in thirty seconds. You need to know how to mime, how to express with just your face."

Often, your audition will be videotaped. Wendy Lee describes an audition in Denver, Colorado: "They give you a small amount of script, maybe thirty seconds. You hand them your headshot, stand on your mark, tell them your name and agency." Then you read your lines.

It's hard to get up a lot of enthusiasm in a situation like that, but here's a trick: try to forget you're performing to a camera. Picture an enthusiastic audience sitting across from you. Now go for it!

## Television and Film

For TV situation comedy or soap opera auditions, try to memorize the lines you've been given. Television shows are filmed on a tight schedule, and the director doesn't have much time to work with the actors. Therefore, the casting director will want to see that you can deliver the lines without a lot of preparation or coaching.

Producer/ director James Stanfield auditioned dozens of young actors for his educational video *Be Cool*.

If you're auditioning for a feature film, especially one with a serious theme, you won't be expected to act quite so perky and energetic. Instead, casting directors are looking for depth and discipline. They want to see that you have the acting talent required to create a believable character. "You have to get into the whole film," Judy Belshe explains. "It's not a joke every fifteen seconds. You have to develop the character."

## Plays and Musicals

Theater auditions are a whole different ball game. You will be expected to come prepared with a monologue. If you're trying out for a musical, you will also be asked to sing a song. Theater actors have to project up to the last row of the balcony, so you'll need to speak loudly, put a lot of expression in your voice, and use plenty of dramatic body language.

No matter what you're auditioning for, you shouldn't bury your head in the script. "I want to see acting," declares Judy Belshe. "If you stare at that page, you're only giving me radio."

## I Got a Callback!

If you're called back to audition again, good for you! It means the people in charge liked you enough to want to see you again. Be sure to wear the same clothes you wore to the original audition. It will trigger good memories with the casting director.

Callbacks usually involve more people. The producers or the director might show up to watch you. If you're trying out for a movie or a TV show, you might even be asked to read with the star.

Robyn Richards acted in a TV pilot with Howie Mandel that the network was considering for a new weekly series. "At that point we were down at ABC Television Center," her mother remembers. "There's a huge theater, and all the seats were filled with network people."

Even if you walk in to a callback and find yourself face to face with Kevin Costner, don't panic. Just relax and read your lines exactly the way you did the first time around. After all, it worked before, right?

If the director is present, it's a good idea to show him you can take direction. After you read your lines, look at him and ask, "Would you like me to try it a different way for you?" Listen closely to what he says, then give it your best shot.

★ ★ ★

## Thanks, But No Thanks

No matter how talented an actor you are, you're not going to land every role you audition for. There's not an actor in the world who hasn't experienced the sting of rejection. It's a lousy feeling, but you can't let it get you down.

Eleven-year-old Joanna Hayes has acted in nine plays and thirteen TV commercials. "You have to learn to take rejection in this business," she says in *Kids on Camera*. "I went out to try for the part of Molly in the play *Annie,* but I didn't get it. This was very disappointing for me."

Even big stars blow auditions. Jonathan Jackson, star of *General Hospital* and the film *Camp Nowhere,* told *16,* "Before *Camp Nowhere* came along, I tried out for a movie with Melanie Griffith called *Milk Money.* I really thought I was going to get that part, but I didn't."

The most important thing to remember is that a rejection does not automatically mean you did something wrong. "They're not saying no to *you,*" Judy Belshe emphasizes. "They're saying no to themselves. They've decided it doesn't work for them. It's not personal. They just need something else."

When it comes to auditions, being the right person in the right place at the right time counts for a lot—and that's something you can't control. "If they're looking for a blond, blue-eyed ten-year-old and you happen to be there at that moment, it's fine," explains acting teacher Jan Carter. "If not, you haven't got a chance."

Casting directors aren't going to pat you on the back when you blow an audition. You've got to do that for yourself. After every audition, reward yourself for a job well done. Stop for an ice cream cone on the way home, or buy yourself a new hair ribbon or a pack of baseball cards. When you get home, go into your room, look in the mirror, and tell yourself, "I did a good job!"

## When the Going Gets Tough

No matter how cheerful your outlook is, months of failed auditions can wear you down. Sixteen-year-old Phillip Glasser has acted in over a hundred commercials, but even he has his down times. "I've been to so many auditions where they say, 'Oh, you're perfect for the part. We love you and we want to bring you back.' And then they don't call you back. My mom and I call it the kiss of death."

The solution is to keep a level head about each audition, and to ask your friends and relatives to do the same. Don't convince yourself that you're a shoo-in for the job—the letdown will be twice as hard if you don't get it. On the other hand, don't get down on yourself if an audition didn't go as well as you hoped.

"An audition is a practice session," says agent Monika Simmons. "It's not a life-or-death situation. You do your best, and then you leave it behind. The more auditions you do, the better you will get at your craft. It's important not to become obsessed with each audition."

When you're feeling really discouraged, remind yourself that even a failed audition can lead to bigger and better things. Tiffani-Amber Thiessen tried out for the TV show *Models Inc.,* but didn't land a role. She did, however, make a fabulous impression on the producer, Aaron Spelling. Later, when he was looking for an actress to play the part of Valerie Malone on *Beverly Hills 90210,* he remembered Tiffani—and hired her.

# Up Close and Personal:

# Paul Sutera

Paul Sutera was five years old when he landed his first acting gig—performing in a school play in Orlando, Florida. "I had a tiny, tiny part," he remembers, "but there was something about it . . . I got so into it. I felt special because not everybody got to do it."

By the time the play was over, Paul knew what he wanted to do with his life. He was going to be a professional actor. There was only one problem. His parents had absolutely no intention of letting their son get involved in show business.

"What the media puts out there is frightening," Paul's mother, Joyce, explains. "I'd seen that series of talk shows where they brought out all the [former child stars] that were dysfunctional and I thought, 'This is what Paul wants to do?'"

But he didn't give up. A number of film studios had just opened in the Orlando area, and Paul continually begged his parents to take him to auditions.

Paul Sutera

Finally, Paul's father, Frank, saw an ad in the newspaper about a seminar at the local high school that promised to teach parents everything they needed to know to get children into show business. "Since Paul hadn't dropped the subject," Joyce explains, "my husband said maybe we should just get some information." Little did they know the seminar would change their lives.

One of the speakers that day was Gary Scalzer, a Los Angeles talent manager. After his talk, he invited the children in the audience to read a scene for him. Paul remembers it well. "I read a monologue for Chips Ahoy cookies," he recalls. "When it was all over, he [the manager] asked to speak with my parents. He said, 'I want to take your son to Hollywood.'"

"We said no," Paul's mother remembers. But Scalzer was not discouraged. He referred the Suteras to a local talent agent, who readily agreed to meet Paul. That very day Paul was sent on an audition for the movie *Parenthood*. He read for the casting director, met director Ron Howard, and was called back the next day. Although he ultimately didn't get the part, the experience was an eye-opener for his parents. The next day, they called Gary Scalzer.

"See? I told you," he said. "You've got to bring this kid out here." When Paul's parents still hesitated, he told them, "Just give me six weeks. If nothing happens, I won't bother you anymore."

Things were getting serious. The entire family— Mom, Dad, Paul, brother Frank, and sisters Frances and Suzy—sat down for a family talk. Everyone could see that Paul was dying to go to Hollywood, and everyone felt he should give it a try. And so it was decided. Nine-year-old Paul was about to get a shot at the big time!

A few weeks later Paul and his mother arrived in Los Angeles. Gary Scalzer met them at the airport and took them to the apartment he had found for them. Living in the same building were other families that Scalzer had brought out to Hollywood, including some young actors who would soon become famous—movie star Elijah Wood, *Step by Step*'s Angela Watson, and *Home Improvement*'s Jonathan Taylor Thomas. But when Paul met them, they were all rookies.

"Everybody was brand-new, and we were all friendly," Paul's mom says. "When somebody got an audition, everybody got excited for him. It was a real supportive group."

Soon Paul was sent on his first audition. "I had butterflies in my stomach," he recalls. "I was nervous, but I don't think I showed it."

His mom wasn't as good at hiding her emotions. "I was stressed," she says with a laugh. "He just seemed so calm, and I was afraid my nerves would affect him. So I took my needlework and sat in a corner."

It must have worked, because before long Paul landed his first job—a Mazda commercial. A couple of weeks later, he won another commercial job. Then it was time to return home, where he was faced with a big decision.

Paul's dad, an insurance agent, had recently been transferred to Miami. The family was still living in Orlando while their father commuted. But if Mrs. Sutera was going to continue taking Paul to Hollywood, all that would have to change. "There was no way we could travel back and forth and still maintain the house in Orlando *and* a condo in Miami," she explains. If Paul quit traveling to L.A., his parents decided, they could keep the house in Orlando. Otherwise, they'd have to sell it.

Paul loved the big house and the horse they kept in the backyard. But he loved acting even more. He told his parents he wanted to return to Hollywood. "Knowing how much it meant to him, we felt we had to support him," his mother declares.

That was the start of the Sutera family's new routine. In the spring, Paul and his mother live in Los Angeles while Paul auditions for TV pilots. Dad and the other kids stay home. Then Paul and his mom return to Florida until the fall, when they go to L.A. again so he can audition for guest shots on the new TV shows.

"It's a sacrifice, but it's also been kind of fun," Paul's mother says. But she wouldn't recommend it for everyone. "I've seen a lot of families come out here and split up. It has to really be something you do together. You have to keep the lines of communication open all the time and don't take anything for granted. Our family talks, we talk about everything."

Over the next four years Paul did a TV pilot, commercials, and two feature films. Then, little by little, the offers stopped coming. "There was a time this last year when I got a few voice-overs, but nothing really major," he remembers. "All my friends . . . were getting good-sized parts. For awhile I was really rethinking whether I should keep doing this or not. Because if I'm not getting all that much work, I'd rather stay home and see my friends and be with my family."

But any thoughts of quitting show business disappeared when Paul landed the role of Peter in *The Brady Bunch Movie*. Suddenly, he was hot stuff in

Hollywood. Paramount Pictures signed Paul to a three-film contract, and *The Hollywood Reporter*, a well-known industry newspaper, ran an article on him. In the article, Jenno Topping, one of the producers of *The Brady Bunch Movie*, is quoted as saying, "He has an unusual quality and is at that age where he is sensitive and starting to be sexy."

Next, the fan magazines started calling. "*Bop* and *Big Bopper* interviewed me," Paul says with a hint of embarrassment. "I did a celebrity date thing for *Bop*. Two girls were selected to go on a date with me."

But don't think all the attention has given Paul a swelled head. In fact, he laughs at the thought. "When the magazine brought the idea to me and said, 'Do you want to do this?'" I was thinking, '*Me*?' I had to check to see if anyone was standing behind me!"

How does Paul stay so humble? He shrugs. "When I go back home, if I have any kind of ego my friends will slap me around and say, 'Hey, what's wrong with you?'"

His parents help keep him straight, too. "We've always said, 'The first sign he's a brat, it's over,'" his mother insists.

Clearly, Paul doesn't have to worry. He's got both feet planted firmly on the ground. "The way I look at it, acting is a job," he explains. "It's just like being a doctor or a dentist or anything, except that there's more publicity."

So why does he do it? "For me, it's not the money," he says. "I do it because I get to meet so many great people. I met Michael Landon, Bob Hope, Roseanne . . . It's really something you can learn from and have a lot of fun."

For talented Paul Sutera, the fun is just beginning.

# CHAPTER 7

# I GOT THE PART!

**C**ongratulations—you got the part!

If you're like most young actors, you're probably jumping for joy—and frightened to death. What if the director yells, "Action" and your mind goes blank? What if you walk onstage and fall flat on your face? This job is supposed to be the beginning of a long and brilliant acting career. You don't want to blow your very first chance at stardom.

Relax! It's normal to feel nervous when you're going into a new and

Doing commercials can be hard. You have to say, 'Oh, this is so good!' But sometimes you're stuffed and the product tastes horrible!

*—Actor Olivia Hack*

A tight fit: The man holding the microphone had to stand in a lavatory stall during this scene from the video *Be Cool*.

unknown situation. That's why it pays to have some idea of what to expect and what is expected of you. That way, when the curtain goes up on your professional acting career, you'll be ready to dazzle 'em.

## You're Hired

If you have an agent or a manager, she will call you with the good news that you've landed the part. It's the agent's job to negotiate the contract. When you receive your copy, read it over with your parents. Ask questions about anything you don't understand. You may want to have an entertainment lawyer look it over as well. Don't sign anything until you're satisfied that the contract is legal and fair.

If you land a job without an agent, you'll have to

ask your parents or some other responsible adult to negotiate your contract. If possible, have a lawyer who knows something about entertainment contracts read it over. At the very least, make sure your parents know what a standard show biz contract looks like. The book *So You Want to Get Your Child into Commercials* (see the Bibliography) includes a sample contract.

Your agent or manager will prepare you for the job by sending you a copy of the script (if there is one), and telling you when and where to go and what to bring. You should also find out who your contact person is on the set so you know who to report to. If you don't have an agent, you'll get the information from the casting director, producer, or art director.

In many states you will need to obtain a work permit. Ask your agent or employer how to get one. Often, work permits are coordinated by your local school superintendent's office. It's your stage parent's job to apply for the permit.

There are a few other things you and your stage parent will need to bring to the job: your social security card, a copy of your birth certificate or green card, your passport or other official photo ID card, and your stage parent's driver's license.

Three major unions represent working actors—the Screen Actors Guild, the American Federation of Television and Radio Artists, and the Actors' Equity Association. If this is your first job, you don't need to worry about being a union member. In some states, however, you must join the union within thirty days after your first job in order to land more union jobs.

Other states are "right-to-work" states, which

means you never have to join a union to get acting jobs. The book *So You Want to Get Your Child into Commercials* lists the rules for every state.

## On Your Mark

Once you receive a copy of the script, it's time to get to work. If you're acting in a commercial, you probably don't have to spend much time figuring out your character. Commercials are short and simple, and the personality of the kid you play is going to be pretty straightforward and obvious. The important thing is to learn your lines and to work on using lots of facial expression and body language.

Movies and plays require more preparation. Read the entire script and think about your character. What kind of person is he? What does he want? What is his relationship to the other characters? You may want to dream up a "back story" for your character—that is, what happened to him *before* the script begins. What do you imagine occurred in the past that made him the person he is on page one?

Some actors like to do research on their character. If the script is set in Montana at the turn of the century, you can go to your local library and read about that period in history. If your character is a modern-day paperboy, you might want to interview a kid your age who delivers newspapers. Perhaps you can even join him on his route one day.

Your next big responsibility is to memorize your lines. Read them to yourself, then practice them out loud in front of a mirror. Finally, ask your stage parent or a friend to practice them with you. Remember, it's not enough to just recite the lines. You need to think about your facial expression, your body language, and your character's inner emotions. And don't forget that you're acting even when you aren't speaking. *Listen* when the other characters are talking—and react.

Trying to memorize page after page of dialogue can be an intimidating experience the first time around. Jonathan Taylor Thomas, star of *Home Improvement,* has a forty-plus-page script to learn every week! But after years of practice, he breezes through it. "You have a whole five days to do it," he told *Bop,* "and by the fourth day, you normally have it. Even if they change [your lines] on you and stuff like that, you get the memorization down pat after awhile."

If you're excited about your role—and who wouldn't be on a first job?—learning your lines will be a pleasure, not a chore. "She gets her scripts and she's so excited," says Mary Richards, mother of *General Hospital*'s Robyn Richards. "She runs in, highlights them, and she has them all memorized. I don't even work with her anymore. She does it all by herself."

### *Get Set*

Prepare for your first job exactly the way you did for your first audition. Get a good night's sleep, eat well-balanced meals, and avoid sugar.

On the day of the shoot, show up on time. Even if your agent or employer has told you how long the shoot will last, be prepared to stay all day. Filming almost always ends up taking longer than anticipated. But don't let anyone take advantage of you. There are laws that govern how long a minor can work, and they vary from state to state. Your agent or your state's department of labor can give you the details.

Bring a bag with all the things you'll need to be comfortable—a change of clothes, towels, snacks, quiet toys, books, your homework, and so on. And, of course, don't forget your script!

When you arrive on the set, look for your contact person. Smile, shake hands, and introduce your stage parent. It's important to make a good first impression, just as you did at the audition. After all, you're going to be working with this person all day (in fact, if you're filming a movie, you may be working with her for months!), so you want to get off on the right foot.

## Go!

This is it—the moment you've been waiting for! You're on the set and eager to start acting. What happens next? Well, it all depends on what kind of acting you're going to be doing.

## Print Jobs

The shoot will probably be held in a photographer's studio. Sometimes, however, you will be asked to model on location—on a city street, in a playground, or at the beach, for example.

Matt Jensen, his sister Kristin, and his parents were chosen to do a "concept shoot" (an ad concept submitted to the client for consideration). "They took our picture with a Volkswagen Jetta in a 130-degree airport hangar," Mrs. Jensen says. Eventually, the Jensens were chosen to be Volkswagen's 1995 Jetta family and were photographed on location in Wyoming, South Dakota, Wisconsin, and Minnesota.

At a print job, a great deal of time will be spent getting you ready to be photographed. You'll be trying on clothes while people poke and prod you, spray hair spray at your head, and dab powder on your face.

The photographer will tell you what to do. Your job is to appear relaxed and spontaneous, and to project lots of enthusiasm and personality—even if you're standing under hot lights in a wool coat, or wading in a freezing pond in a bathing suit.

". . . there are the kids who are too trained," writes Macy's fashion art director, Brad Harrison, in *Kids on Camera*. "You can tell that their parents have posed them in front of the mirror for days and days. . . . The 'natural' kids know how to pose, they know how to laugh, they know how to move and not every movement is a forced pose."

When the shoot is finished, your stage parent will be asked to sign a photo release, a form that gives the photographer the right to publish your photograph. Make sure your parent reads the release carefully and doesn't sign away any rights that haven't been discussed and agreed upon before the shoot.

## Commercials

Commercial shoots can be very intense. "Money is a big deal," writes producer Lisa Donini in *Kids on Camera*. "You can be dealing with a lot of money that can be misappropriated between the initial idea and what actually ends up on film." There are also a lot of people involved—the director, the producer, the advertising executives, the client—and they all have a say in what the final product will look like.

Naturally, with so much money at stake and so many different personalities involved, things are going to get a little tense from time to time. Try not to take it personally. Listen to the director and do what he tells you. And keep smiling.

Commercials are filmed in a TV studio or on location. "Don't plan anything the day of the shoot other than the commercial," Donini warns. "Not only that day, but that night. The parents should make sure the child knows that he will have to wait a lot."

Be prepared to perform the same small scene over and over again. Phillip Glasser remembers his experience filming a waffle commercial. "I'll never eat a frozen waffle again!" he exclaims. "I ate like three hundred of them, and they had all this gook on them." If you do have to bite a piece of food repeatedly, there will be a "spit bucket" available for you to spit the food into after each take. It may sound gross, but it's better than trying to stuff down dozens of candy bars or bologna sandwiches.

Commercials can be hard work, but they can also be a real blast. "I had the most fun doing a commercial for White Water, a water amusement park," says eleven-year-old Nate Schuman in *Kids on Camera,* "because I got to go on the rides during the commercial, and I also got a free pass."

### Television

Many weekly television shows, especially situation comedies, are filmed before a live audience. Rider Strong, star of *Boy Meets World,* describes the process in *Bop*: "Well, Thursday night we get a new script, and Friday morning we read it. You know, all the actors sit down at the table, and we read the script together and then we block the scenes [plan out how the actors will move on the set and what props they will use]. . . . On

121

Hurry up and wait: Shawn Toovey and his mother waiting around between scenes on the set of *Dr. Quinn, Medicine Woman*.

Monday, we block scenes more. . . . Every day we get more script changes, with jokes that work and jokes that don't work. They change it constantly.

"Tuesday we keep blocking, and then Wednesday they bring in the camera and we block with the camera, because the cameras have to move constantly, too. Thursday, we come in about twelve o'clock or one o'clock in the afternoon, and we tape [in front of an audience] that night."

Don't expect to receive much input from the director. He's working on a very tight schedule and doesn't have a lot of time to work with the actors. A TV director's main job is to block the scenes and make sure they're shot correctly.

During filming the cast tries to get through an entire scene without stopping. If someone makes a

122

mistake, they start over from the beginning, and the audience is asked to react as if they were seeing the scene for the first time.

If the show isn't filmed live, fewer cameras will probably be used. A master shot of the entire scene will be shot first, followed by reaction shots (a reaction shot shows a character's reaction to another character's dialogue or action).

On the set, your dressing room will be a trailer. Don't expect luxury. Even *seaQuest DSV* heartthrob Jonathan Brandis has a trailer just big enough to hold a couch, a small table, and a mini-kitchenette. "They all look like this," he told *16*, "except Roy's [Roy Scheider, the star of the show]—his is really a motor home. It's really luxurious!"

Every week, you will receive a call schedule (a sheet that tells you what scenes you are in and when you need to report to work). If you're the star of the show, you may appear in every scene, and that can mean some long days. If you have a smaller part, you can kick back. "We tease each other," says Angela Watson, discussing her co-stars on the ensemble show *Step by Step*. "If one guy has a big part and I have a few lines I can cruise on in at three o'clock."

On a successful series the cast and crew becomes your second family. After all, you'll probably be spending as much time on the set—if not more—than you spend at home! If you're a guest star on a series, you may feel a bit like an outsider. Don't act offended or show off to get attention. If you do a good job and make people like you, you may impress the producers so much that they decide to add your character to the series. If that happens, you've got it made.

## Films

Feature films are shot in movie studios or on location. Since moviemakers want their films to look authentic, they often travel to many far-flung locales to film. Sometimes it's the place actually described in the script; sometimes it's a place that can double for the real thing. For example, many films set in New York City are actually shot in Toronto.

Movies take much longer to film than commercials or TV shows—sometimes as long as six months. The smaller the budget, the tighter the production schedule.

Before filming begins the director will probably bring all the actors together to rehearse. You'll sit in a room, getting to know each other and reading the script out loud. You may even improvise together, or simply chat. The idea is to get comfortable with each other.

Shooting a movie can be very intense. You're together with the same people every day for months on end. It also involves long hours. Every scene in the film has to be shot many times from several different angles, including a wide shot, and plenty of close-ups of each character.

Moviemaking can also be great fun, especially when lots of kids are involved. Listen to Jonathan Jackson describing the *Camp Nowhere* set to the readers of *16*: "The whole cast just joked around constantly. We played football and all hung out together. All of us kids had a great time getting to know each other and working together."

Sometimes things can get a little wild, too. ". . . every time somebody falls asleep, there's shaving cream on their face when they wake up," Vincent La Russo told *16* about the set of *Mighty Ducks II*. "We're really into pranks like that."

## Voice-over Work

Many young actors find work just using their voices. Actors provide the voices for the characters in animated TV shows, movies, and commercials. They are also used to supply extra voices that are added to previously filmed scenes, such as background voices in a restaurant scene or a crowd scene.

Sometimes the makers of a movie or commercial are unhappy with the voice of one of the actors, so a new actor is brought in to replace the original actor's voice. The job is a tricky one because you must watch the film and dub in the dialogue to match the original actor's moving lips.

Phillip Glasser provided the voice of Fievel in the movie *An American Tail* and is in constant demand as a voice-over actor. He loves the laid-back nature of the work. "You just show up," he says. "You don't have to be dressed nice. It's relaxed."

Voice-over work can feel a little impersonal—you're often sitting alone in a recording booth with headphones on—and it probably won't make you famous. On the other hand, it's often a breeze. Ari Gold, a young actor who has done over three hundred and fifty jingles and voice-overs, describes his work in a one-and-a-half-minute commercial. "When the time was right, I said, 'Delicious,'" he writes in *The Young Performer's Guide,* "and from that one take I made four thousand dollars."

★　★　★

## Theater

If you've been hired to act in a play or musical, you'll have weeks of rehearsal before your first performance. Rehearsals will probably be held in the theater where the play will be staged, or in a rehearsal hall attached to the theater.

Early rehearsals will involve sitting around a table with the cast, reading through the script. If it's a long play and you have a lot of lines, the director won't expect you to have your entire part memorized yet. At the end of the first rehearsal, you'll be given a due date for when you must be "off-book" (able to rehearse without a script in your hand).

The next few weeks of rehearsal will mostly be spent blocking. As the blocking progresses, you'll get a chance to spend more and more time working on the actual acting. Listen carefully to the director's suggestions and don't be afraid to ask questions.

The last week of rehearsals is called production week. Light and sound cues will be added into the show. A day or two before opening night, you'll have a dress rehearsal—a chance for the cast to run through the entire show in costume. Then, at long last, the curtain goes up, and it's show time.

Theater is very demanding because, except for intermission, there are no breaks between scenes. You're performing the play from beginning to end, in front of a live audience. But that's what makes it so exciting.

"The most fun thing I've ever done in this business was when I played the part of Annie," Joanna Hayes says in *Kids on Camera*. "I did seventy-one shows in all. My mom would ask me how I could stand getting up there and doing a great job seventy-one times. It is important to me how my performance affects an audience. I like to see their reaction. It was a different audience every night. It gave me the energy."

## Straight from the Heart

Acting is hard work because you're expected to express all sorts of deep emotions on cue, under bright lights, while the director and the crew look on. "The hardest thing I did was working on the TV series [*Rescue*] *911*," says eight-year-old Katy Schuman in *Kids on Camera*. "I had to pretend I stabbed somebody, and it was kind of hard to get into."

Acting in TV and movies can be especially difficult because the script is usually shot out of sequence. For example, all the scenes set in the same location will probably be filmed at the same time. As a result, you could end up acting in the last scene of the movie on the first day of filming.

The trick is to keep track of where you are in the script. The director will help you, and you can also discuss each scene with your stage parent as you rehearse your lines. Professional actors learn to lose themselves in the emotions of every scene. You can do it, too. Forget about the bright lights, your too-tight costume, and the bored-looking guy behind the camera. Just concentrate on what's happening in the script and make it come alive.

Paul Sutera has a method that helps him act in emotional scenes. When he needs to cry on cue, he says, "I think of sad moments in my life, like when my horse was sold and I had to move away from all my friends. I just bring one of those memories out and that helps me."

Robyn Richards has a simple explanation when asked how she gets into character for her role on *General Hospital*. "I just feel like I'm in Maxie's shoes," she says.

In general, your job is to follow the script and not change a word unless the director tells you to. Sometimes, however, a little improvising can make the difference between a so-so performance and an outstanding one.

Casting director Nancy Smith remembers a recycling commercial she worked on. "The closing shot is Grandpa pulling his grandson in a little red wagon," she says. "Well, it was going to be the kid sitting facing Grandpa, but suddenly he turned around and smiled at the camera—and it was wonderful! Kids are very spontaneous, and sometimes the things they do are better than what the director planned."

If you have an idea for improving your performance, try it in rehearsal. If the director responds positively, go for it. If not, return to the script and follow it to the letter. Remember, when you're acting, the director is the boss.

## Behind the Scenes

If you're working on a union job during the school year and are hired for three or more days, the production company will provide a tutor to teach you and the other young actors on the job. School will probably be held in a trailer on the set. You are required by law to receive three hours of tutoring every day.

The teacher on the set also functions as a welfare worker. It's his job to make sure you are working only as long as the labor laws allow, and that you are safe and well cared for at all times. Most welfare workers do a good job, but sometimes they miss things. That's why it's important for your stage parent to be with you on the set at all times.

In general, your stage parent is expected to stay out of the way and keep quiet when you're rehearsing or filming. But if you're being mistreated, that's a different story. Then it's your parent or guardian's responsibility to speak up.

Mea Hack remembers the time her daughter Olivia was doing a commercial for a chain of national fast-food restaurants. "The director was not good with children," she says. "He was abusive. And Olivia said, 'I don't want to do this.'"

Mea responded by standing at the edge of the set and giving the director a stern look whenever he was unkind to Olivia. Finally, he got the message and took Mea aside to talk to her. She told him what was wrong in no uncertain terms.

"He wasn't defensive," she recalls with a smile. "He was mortified. After that, he totally changed his style and it was fine."

### It's a Wrap

You did it! You finished your first honest-to-goodness modeling or acting job. Give yourself a pat on the back. Now it's time to start auditioning again. But this time around you'll have more experience *and* a new listing on your resume. So go out there and strut your stuff. You're a professional now!

# CHAPTER  8

# MAKING YOUR MOVE TO THE BIG TIME

**Y**our first professional job is a happy memory. You did an outstanding job, made some contacts, and improved your resume. Soon you land another job, and another, and another. Pretty soon, local casting directors and art directors are calling and asking for *you*.

Suddenly, you're in demand. You're making money. The checkout girl at the grocery store recognizes you from a commercial you did for cable TV. In short, you're a local celebrity.

New York and L.A. are where most of the motion pictures and the big stuff are done. That was just a dream. It really never [seemed] conceivable.

—*Jonathan Taylor Thomas, star of* Home Improvement, *in* Bop

What now? Do you coast along, enjoying your success? Or do you risk it all for a shot at national stardom? The answer is up to you.

## Big Fish in a Small Pond

There's nothing wrong with staying local, at least until you finish high school. That's what *Beverly Hills 90210* heartthrob Luke Perry did. His mother asked him to stay in school in Ohio until he turned eighteen. After graduation rolled around, he and a few of his buddies packed up and headed for Hollywood.

Paul Petersen, who acted on *The Donna Reed Show* as a child, believes kids should wait even longer. "What's wrong with having a child working in community theater and in high school productions?" he asks. "Education comes first, and if they want to be an actor at age twenty-two when they finish college, fine."

Brain Gaskill, who played David on *Models Inc.,* did exactly that. After graduating from the State University of New York and performing in a Cleveland, Ohio, production of the play *The Lion in Winter,* he moved to Hollywood. Three months later, he auditioned for *Models Inc.* and landed the role.

Some young actors are happy to continue acting locally. "I'm happy doing stuff here," says twelve-year-old Santa Barbara, California, actor Noah Gaines. "I used to go down to L.A. for auditions, but it got really frustrating. You drive down there for two hours and then you're in a big room with a sea of kids and parents."

Even if auditioning wasn't so frustrating, Noah still wouldn't pin all his hopes on an acting career. "I don't think I'd want to do this as a profession because it's not very steady," he says. "You can have three jobs in a row and then nothing for two years."

According to *The Los Angeles Agent Book,* there are 76,000 members of the Screen Actors Guild and on any given day 75 percent of them are unemployed. Do you think you can beat the odds and become a star? If you're willing to take a chance, read on.

## Small-Town Discoveries

It *is* possible to land a big-time job without moving to Los Angeles or New York, even if you don't have an agent. "The casting agents do get around," says Ed Ims, director of Showbiz Kids. "They'll find people in remote and odd locations. But the casting directors usually only appear at public functions, so the child performer has to get exposure if they're going to attract interest."

That means performing in community theater or local talent shows. Mario Lopez (*Saved by the Bell, Choose Your Own Adventure*), for example, was discovered at a dance contest in San Diego when he was only ten years old.

Sometimes Hollywood producers will hire a local casting director to find young talent for a specific role, as was done for the movie *A Home of Our Own*, starring Kathy Bates. The producers hired Salt Lake City, Utah, casting director Cate Praggastis to cast four of the six children's roles.

"We didn't have the budget for a nationwide search, so they were cast in Salt Lake City, where the picture was shot," explains director Tony Bill in *Parade Magazine.* "I'm very proud of them. None had any acting experience."

But the odds of being plucked from obscurity to play a role in a Hollywood movie are small. You have a better chance of landing a national job if you have an agent in a midsized city who is getting you local work.

"Casting companies in bigger markets will contact us because they want to find new kids," explains Denver agent Wendy Lee. "Like the little girl who played the young girlfriend in [the movie] *Forrest Gump* they found in Aspen [Colorado]."

Hollywood agents and managers also search the country for young actors. "Someone from one of the big agencies in L.A. came out looking for kids," Wendy Lee remembers. "He wanted me to put together my ten best child actors. He put them on tape and took them back to L.A. If any of those children get work in L.A., we get 5 percent [commission] because we're the mother agency."

Small-city agents subscribe to the breakdown service, just as New York and Hollywood agents do. If one of their clients seems right for a particular role, they can submit a video audition. Kansas City, Missouri, agent Dave Jackson, for example, learned that Cybill Shepherd was looking for young actors to play her daughter in a TV show, *Cybill*. "We had the sides from the script and we had the kids make a videotape," he says. "We maybe submitted thirty girls for those parts."

### Going Where the Work Is

Yes, it is possible to be discovered in your hometown, but don't count on it. "The only time that happens is when they're looking for very specific, unusual types—like for the *Little Rascals* movie,"

133

claims Arizona agent Monika Simmons. "Then they will do a national search. But for the everyday opportunities that come up in L.A. or New York, you have to be there."

Even when a national commercial is cast locally, the odds of landing a role are slim. Laura Jensen describes what happens to her son, Matt: "He's only had four, maybe five auditions that weren't for catalogs. And when there is an audition for a national commercial, it's a cattle call and everyone in town shows up—even people who don't have an agent but heard about it through a friend. It's crazy."

Matt feels he needs an L.A. agent. Agent Kimberly Johnson agrees. "There are those one-in-a-million kids that will be discovered. It doesn't matter where they are, someone will find them. But on the whole, there are millions of cute kids everywhere. If you don't live there [in Los Angeles or New York], you won't get those jobs."

But just try convincing your parents of that! They aren't going to quit their jobs, sell the house, and move to Hollywood or New York just because you've got stars in your eyes. Or are they?

Jonathan Brandis grew up in Connecticut and began modeling at the age of two. By age six, he had acted in TV commercials in New York and on the soap opera *One Life to Live*. When Jonathan was nine, his family moved to Los Angeles so he could have a shot at the big time. His mother became his manager, and his father bought a food distributorship. Soon Jonathan was landing small parts in TV series and movies. Next came *seaQuest DSV*, and stardom.

But most families aren't so quick to abandon their

old lives and start over again in a big, unknown city. And why should they? The chances that you'll become a rich, famous actor are a million to one.

So how are you going to convince Mom and Dad to give you a shot at stardom? By proving to them you don't have to move to New York or Los Angeles to try out for major roles—you just have to visit.

### Before You Go

It's just about impossible to find work in New York or Hollywood without an agent—especially if you're only planning to be there for a short time. If you have a local agent, ask her if she can recommend a big-city agent for you. If she has connections in Hollywood or the Big Apple, she might be able to find an agent for you fairly easily.

If you don't have a local agent, or if your agent can't recommend someone, then it's up to you to find a big-city agent. If you're planning on traveling to L.A., send for a list of SAG-franchised agents (see Chapter Five). New York agents and casting directors are listed in *The Ross Report* (send $3.50 to 40-29 27th Street, Long Island City, NY 11101). Find out who handles children, then send out your headshot and resume.

"I will look at pictures sent to me from anywhere in the country," says Barbara Laga, a talent agent with Ford Models in New York, in *Kids on Camera*. "They do not have to go through another agency, a modeling conference, or a modeling school. If they include a SASE [self-addressed, stamped envelope], we will respond back to them."

But is a photo and resume enough to get you

noticed? Casting director Bob Anthony keeps thousands of photos and resumes stacked in his office. "Most people are overwhelmed when they see these," he says in *The Young Performer's Guide*. "It gives them pause when they realize that most casting directors receive in a year an amount that equals, if not surpasses, what we keep here."

A videotape of your work can prove to an agent that you have talent and that you look good on film. The video should include at least three different pieces that show off your range of talent. They can be clips from something you actually performed in (a commercial, a play, a movie), or you can hire someone to film you performing some monologues or scenes. The video should be no more than ten to twelve minutes long.

"Tape is sight, sound, and motion," Bob Anthony declares. "Nothing is as powerful."

## Your Big-Apple Bash

Summer is the season for young actors to visit New York. You probably won't get hired for a TV series, since most of them are filmed in L.A., but lots of commercial jobs are available. In July the fall and back-to-school ads are being cast. In August the industry is gearing up for Christmas commercials. Young actors are in demand, but many of the local child actors are on vacation or away at summer camp.

"A fresh face in summer is a novelty for the casting people," writes New York agent Tina Pentimone in *The Young Performer's Guide*. "They're not seeing the same kids that come to call after call throughout the year. The kids from far away are the new kids, which is probably why they book so much over the summer."

If you have a close family friend or a relative in New York, so much the better. You'll have a place to stay (a huge advantage, since apartments and hotels are very expensive) and someone to show you around the city. In fact, if your friend or relative is willing to take you to auditions, then your stage parent doesn't need to come to New York at all. That's a big plus if you have brothers or sisters who need to be cared for, or if your stage parent is having trouble taking time off from her job.

If you don't have friends or relatives in the city, ask your New York agent or manager to suggest places to stay. He may know another young actor who would be willing to rent an apartment with you.

Even if you live within driving distance of New York, leave your car at home. Traffic is heavy, and it's hard to find parking spaces. In Manhattan, public transportation is the way to go.

If you're trying out for a play in New York, be prepared for some stiff competition. Good looks and natural charm aren't enough to land a role. Theater directors want children who are trained actors. For musical roles, outstanding singing and dancing also is required.

Jean Page recalls the summer she brought her children, Susie and Chris, to New York. The local child actors they met at auditions were extremely well-trained and well-prepared, and their mothers seemed to know show business inside and out. Despite the stiff competition, Susie and Chris Page both found summer work in New York. They didn't become famous, but they made some money—and during their off hours, they had the chance to see lots of Broadway shows.

## Your Hollywood Holiday

Hollywood is the place to go if you dream of landing a role in a television show. The best times to visit L.A. are during pilot season (when the new TV pilots are being cast), and episode season (when guest stars are being cast for the new fall shows). Pilot season lasts for three months in the spring, and episode season runs three months in the fall. If you can only come to Hollywood in the summer, you'll be reading mostly for commercials and movie roles.

Once again, you have an advantage if you can stay with a friend or relative in the area. If you don't know anyone, ask your Hollywood agent or manager for advice on where to stay. You want to be close to the studios and the casting directors' offices so that you don't have a long drive to auditions. Most show business activity does not take place within the Hollywood city limits but rather in the San Fernando Valley—in towns like Encino, Burbank, and Studio City. It's a big area, so plan on bringing or renting a car.

Many famous stars began their careers with a short trip to Los Angeles. "I was living in Sacramento, doing modeling and local commercials in San Francisco," Jonathan Taylor Thomas told *Bop*. "L.A. was so farfetched . . . well, not farfetched, but it was just like a dream, you know?"

But when a family friend suggested that nine-year-old Jonathan look for work in L.A., his mother, Claudine, took him there on a trial basis. Not long after they arrived, he landed the role of Kevin Brady in the short-lived series *The Bradys*. After that, his family moved to L.A. permanently, and within a year, Jonathan was picked to play Randy on *Home Improvement*.

Tia and Tamera Mowry were modeling and entering beauty pageants in Texas when they decided they wanted to be TV stars. "We saw all the little actors and actresses on TV and we said, 'Mom, that looks like fun. Let's do *that*!'" they told *People*.

Their mother made a deal with them. If the girls could land a TV commercial within a month, she would move the family to California. They agreed, and so in the summer of 1988 she took a thirty-day leave from her Army job and headed to Glendale, California, to stay with friends. Within a month, Tia and Tamera were hired for a Chrysler commercial. True to her word, their mother resigned from the military and moved permanently to Los Angeles in 1989.

After that, the girls (and their little brother, Tahj) got parts on *Full House*. That led to their big break—producer Irene Dreayer created the series *Sister, Sister* specifically for them.

## To Move or Not to Move

Even if you do manage to land work in New York or Hollywood, your family members may not be willing to give up their old lives and move to the Coast—at least not immediately.

Listen to *General Hospital* star Jonathan Jackson: "We live in Washington and came down to Los Angeles a few years ago to visit our aunt," he told *16*. "We went to Universal Studios and got picked to act in this *Back to the Future* exhibit."

Jonathan and his brother were bitten by the acting bug, but their family wasn't about to leave Washington right away. The boys returned home, found an agent,

Paul Sutera, relaxing outside his Los Angeles condo. He spends half the year in L.A. and half in Florida.

and began doing local commercials and modeling.

"Every once in a while, we'd come to Los Angeles and try out for bigger roles," he explains. It wasn't until he landed a part on *General Hospital* that he and his family decided to stay.

Some child stars never permanently move to L.A. or New York. *Dr. Quinn* star Shawn Toovey lives with his mother and father in a condo near the set, but he returns to his family home in Texas whenever he has a vacation.

*General Hospital* actor Robyn Richards lives ninety miles from Hollywood in the house she grew up in. She and her family have no plans to move to L.A. "We're happy with what we're doing," says her mother. "We live here, we can have a life *and* do the soap opera. We don't want to move."

# Up Close and Personal:

## Angela Watson

Can a farm girl from small-town Illinois find success and happiness in glamorous, glittery Hollywood? If the girl is nineteen-year-old Angela Watson, star of the ABC-TV series *Step by Step*, the answer is a resounding *yes*! But back in Danville, Illinois, Angela didn't dream of a career in show business. "I always wanted to be a scientist or a lawyer," she insists.

Still, she did have a flair for performing. She took tap-dancing lessons from the age of three, and her mother, Barbara, recalls, "We'd have company over and she would show them her tap routines." Her beauty was apparent right from the start, too. "People always told us that someday she'd be Miss America," her mother says. "She was so pretty and sweet."

When Angela was eleven, her father, Allen, a farmer, retired. Looking to escape the snow, he moved his family (including Angela's sister and brother) to

Angela Watson

Cape Coral, Florida. Angela and her mother were at the local mall one day when they saw an advertisement for the Miss Sunburst beauty pageant. "Mom said, 'Wouldn't that be fun?'" Angela remembers. "I wasn't really doing anything else, so I said, 'Yes.' I entered—it was just a little preliminary thing—and I won."

That was the beginning of a beauty-pageant career that kept Angela busy almost every weekend. Soon she was winning state and national trophies right and left, in categories that ranged from beauty to swimwear to winter wear. The only category that gave her trouble was the talent competition. But Angela was determined to change that.

"At first I did tap dancing," she says, "but a singer would almost always beat a dancer. So I decided, 'I'm going to be a singer.'"

Angela's mother was skeptical. Her daughter had never sung in public before. But Angela didn't let that stop her. "I went and bought a Patsy Cline tape," she recalls. "I was going to sing 'Crazy' but it was too hard. Then I heard 'Walking After Midnight' and decided I was going to sing that. So I went in my room for a week—the pageant was that weekend—and I practiced."

Getting onstage to sing her first song wasn't easy for Angela. "When I'm acting, I never get nervous," she says, "but sometimes I did when I was singing. I wasn't always confident of my voice back then." But despite her fears, Angela won the contest. From that moment on, she was a singer.

Angela eventually went on to win over two hundred beauty pageant trophies. But being a winner wasn't all fun and games. "There was a lot of jealousy and competition," she says. "There was one girl especially— we were really good friends at the beginning. And then she grew to hate me because she could never win. She would say nasty things to me. It was kind of sad."

When Angela was twelve, she decided to go to modeling school, mostly because she hoped it would help her win more and bigger beauty pageants. She did so well at the Fort Myers Modeling Connection that she landed a job in New York City modeling a new line of Gotex Swimwear. "It was a big runway show, and it was on HBO," she says. "They brought in all of these models from Europe. There were probably lots of famous ones there, and I didn't even know it."

That show turned out to be Angela's one and only modeling job. When she was thirteen, she competed in a Face Finders Model Search in Dallas, Texas, and won Model of the Year. She had an offer to model in Japan, but when a Hollywood manager approached her and suggested she move to L.A., she changed her mind. "I didn't really want to go to Japan, not knowing anyone there," she explains. "So I decided I wanted to give Hollywood a shot."

Angela's parents were eager to make their daughter's dreams come true, but they weren't about to pick up and move to Los Angeles. They had just built a brand-new home in Florida, and they liked it there. "We were all for it," Barbara Watson recalls, "but in the back of our minds we were thinking, *California?* There was a lot of strangeness to it."

In the end they agreed to take Angela to Hollywood for three or four months and see what happened. Her new manager found them a place to stay and enrolled Angela in acting and commercial classes. Soon she was going on auditions. It was a new experience for her.

"In the pageants I had all this makeup on, and my hair was always curled and filled with hair spray," she explains. "Then I came out here and got my hair cut. I didn't put any hair spray on it, and no makeup because the casting people hate that."

The hardest auditions, she recalls, were the ones in which the casting directors brought in a bunch of kids and told them to "just talk as if you're friends."

"That's the part I hated," she says. "When I was around people I really knew I could be like that, but in auditions I would feel so shy."

She must have done better than she remembers, because soon she landed a role in a McDonald's commercial. Angela will never forget the job, which involved sitting in a McDonald's, eating lunch. "We did [the shot] about thirty or forty times," she moans.

Commercials for Doritos, IBM, and GTE Cordless Phones followed, and Angela's parents decided to take the plunge and move to L.A. Then Angela got a chance to audition for a new TV series called *Davis Rules,* starring Randy Quaid and Jonathan Winters. After one callback, she was hired to play the girlfriend of Randy Quaid's TV son.

For Angela, memorizing the script was a breeze. "I had been in a couple of plays at school," she says. "I usually memorize things really fast." The challenging part was playing opposite wacky comedian Jonathan Winters. "If I had a line that came after his in the scene, I'd really have to listen because he'd ramble on and make up stuff," she recalls with a laugh.

When Angela was fifteen, *Davis Rules* was canceled. Luckily, she wasn't out of work for long. "One day Bob Boyett, the producer of *Step by Step,* called me into his office," she explains. "He had seen me on *Davis Rules,* so I didn't even have to audition or go through a casting director. And I got the part."

Angela landed the role of Karen Foster, the fashionable, self-centered daughter of Suzanne Somers and stepdaughter of Patrick Duffy. "There isn't any person who doesn't go with the flow," she says of the large cast. "When we're off for a week, we miss each other. We're like a real family."

Her favorite episode is one in which she got a chance to show off her singing and dancing skills. "The writers look at what we like to do," she says, "so they had a show where Suzanne Somers and I entered a mother-daughter beauty pageant. We sang 'Boogie Woogie Bugle Boy' and did a tap dance."

When *Step by Step* became a hit, Angela became a star. "People used to mistake me for Danica McKellar, the girl on *The Wonder Years,*" she says. "They'd say, 'Are you Winnie?' Then it changed and they started to ask me, 'Are you Karen?'" Now she gets recognized at the mall, and the fan mail is pouring in.

But with stardom comes responsibility. "I feel like I skipped over the ages of fourteen to eighteen," she says of her busy acting schedule. "You don't have a lot of time to just hang with your friends and do high-school stuff."

It also means you don't have a lot of time for boyfriends. "That's the hardest part," she admits. "You meet guys on the set or at celebrity benefits. But other actors are busy with their own thing. It's hard to meet people."

Still, Angela wouldn't have it any other way. "I went to Disneyland and I was in the line for Space Mountain," she recalls. "Five lines across, three girls yelled out, 'Oh, there's the girl from *Step by Step.*' I was signing autographs back and forth for everybody. It was fun."

Being a TV star is a blast, but Angela looks forward to the day when she can play someone other than pretty, self-centered Karen. "I'd like to do movies and break out of that mold," she says. "I just switched agents because my old agent wasn't sending me out for movie roles. I'm taking a new acting class, too. You have to be eighteen to be in the class. It's really intense, but I love it."

And then there's her blossoming country-music career. "I went to Nashville last year and recorded seven songs," she says eagerly. She also got her feet wet performing at a Strawberry Festival in California. Currently, her manager is trying to land a recording deal for her.

Last year Angela graduated from high school, thanks to a combination of public school and on-set tutoring. Her future plans include acting, singing, *and* finding Mr. Right. "If I found the right person I wouldn't mind getting married at a young age," she confides.

But don't expect Angela to give up her career. "I just love to perform and get up onstage," she exclaims. And luckily for her many fans, that's just what she intends to do.

# CHAPTER 9

# TAMING THE BIG EGO

Suppose it really happens. Suppose you land a role in a hit TV series or a smash motion picture and become hugely famous. Make no mistake about it—your life will change dramatically. How you deal with those changes is up to you. Will you take your fame in stride and remain a normal, happy kid? Or will you turn into a spoiled brat with an ego the size of the Empire State Building?

It's easier to deal with the pressures of stardom

Actors and rock stars are treated like gods in our culture, and some begin to think they're beyond reproach. They're often charming, talented people who just weren't raised right.

—*Actor Eric Stoltz, in the* Los Angeles Times

if you're prepared for them. So sit back, close your eyes, and imagine for a moment that you're one of the most popular young actors in America. What will your life be like? Who will your friends be? Where will you go to school? What will you do in your spare time?

Here are a few facts about fame and fortune that will help you imagine your life as a star:

## Nowhere to Run, Nowhere to Hide

When you're famous, everybody knows who you are. You can't go to the mall or the beach and expect to be left alone. You can't even go to the convenience store for a pack of gum without people pointing and staring.

At first, being recognized can be a thrill. It's fun to have people gaze at you with awe, and it's especially cool when members of the opposite sex swoon over you. But after a while, all that attention can really be a drag.

Picture yourself eating out in a restaurant with your family. The people at the other tables are craning their necks to stare at you. When you take a big bite of your burger and juice runs downs your chin, you can hear the kids around you whispering, "Did you see that? Look at her, she's such a slob!"

Doesn't sound like much fun. But in fact, most fans aren't content to just watch and whisper. They want to talk to their idols, get their autographs, or even hug and kiss them!

"I was in Rochester, New York, in October of 1993 filming the beginning of Luke and Laura's return to *General Hospital*," Jonathan Jackson told *Bop*. "Outside the set there were about two hundred fans. . . . I went over to sign some autographs, and all of a sudden they all came around me!"

David Cassidy, who starred in the TV series *The Partridge Family* from 1970 to 1974, knows that being a teen heartthrob can wear you down. "It was exciting for about the first year, to be the object of so much attention," he writes in his autobiography *C'Mon, Get Happy.* "The fans clustering outside the studio gates morning and night was becoming a problem for me, though . . . Security at my home became an issue, too. There were women showing up, unannounced, uninvited, at all hours."

After awhile you begin to wish everyone would just leave you alone. "It's nice to be recognized," Jonathan Taylor Thomas told *Bop.* But sometimes, he admits, the attention can become "obnoxious."

Shawn Toovey's mother agrees. "Every time someone recognizes us, it takes away a little bit of our privacy," she says.

## Stay Young, Grow Up

It's a big responsibility to be a child star. Producers and directors expect young actors to work at the same pace as the adult actors. You can't goof off just because you're a kid.

"It's intense," says Olivia Hack of her experience working on the films *Star Trek Generations* and *The Brady Bunch Movie.* "You don't have any rest time. You have to keep up the pace."

Alan Simon is the president of a tutoring service for child performers. "On the set, the project comes first, and often there is no room for mistakes," he explains in *The Young Performer's Guide.* "This

Shawn Toovey's school is a trailer on the set of *Dr. Quinn, Medicine Woman.*

directly contradicts what we teach our children; that is, to learn by trial and error."

Young stars learn that although they are playing the role of a child, they are expected to behave like adults. "It makes you mature," says Paul Sutera, "because they're paying you to act younger on camera, but to act twenty years older than you are [off-camera]."

Not only do your employers expect you to be mature, but your fans expect it, too. "At heart I was still a teenager," David Cassidy writes in his autobiography. "But I'd been given a variety of adult responsibilities . . . I knew I had fans looking up to me, expecting me to have answers for everything—often to a degree I found uncomfortable. I mean, I certainly didn't have all the answers!"

Apparently young stars have always been forced to

grow up fast. Listen to Shirley Temple, a famous child star in the 1930s: "I stopped believing in Santa Claus when I was six. Mother took me to see him in a department store, and he asked for my autograph."

## Friends Till the End?

Picture yourself on the set of a big-budget movie filming on location. You're working hard and loving it. Only one problem. You're the only kid in the movie. When the director yells, "Cut!" you have no one to hang out with except adults. When each working day ends, the adult actors get together and party. You sit in your motel room, watching TV and playing solitaire.

Sound tough? It is. Normal kids spend a lot of time going to school and hanging out with their friends. Child stars often bounce back and forth between regular school and on-set tutoring. It's hard to make friends that way, and even harder to stay close to the friends you have.

"I just got an invitation to my friend's fifteenth birthday party," Paul Sutera said recently. "She's Cuban and their fifteenth birthday is like our sweet sixteen. I was supposed to be her escort. I had told her back in seventh grade I'd do it. But I'm out here making a film, so I can't."

And then there's the jealousy factor. Luke Edwards, star of the movie *Little Big League*, told *16*, "Sometimes in public school, kids get jealous."

When your own family gets jealous, it can really make you feel bad. "I think I hurt their feelings sometimes," Matt Jensen says of his brothers and sisters. "Once we got a call and they said, 'We want

Stephen.' He was all excited because that would have been his first job. But then they called back and said they'd made a mistake—they wanted me. He was really bummed out."

## Big Star, Big Ego

*Blossom* star Joey Lawrence was once attacked by three thousand screaming girls at a shopping mall. With adulation like that, how can you keep from getting a swelled head? It isn't easy.

Casting director Judy Belshe has dealt with a few stuck-up kids in her time. She explains, "There's a fallacy that says, 'If everybody knows who I am and everybody sees what I do and everybody likes my talent, then I must be better than everybody else.' But that's just not the truth."

Still, it's hard for young actors not to feel special. "After a show you're on top of the world," Noah Gaines explains. "Everyone is coming up and complimenting you."

Fame can be especially troubling for kids who once thought of themselves as nerds. "I never thought of myself as good-looking until I was in the movies," film star Ethan Hawke (*Reality Bites*) admits. "Nobody else ever thought I was good-looking until I was in the movies."

*Melrose Place* star Heather Locklear knows how he feels. "When I look in the mirror, I see the girl I was growing up—with braces, crooked teeth, a baby face, and a skinny body," she told *People*.

Going from ugly duckling (at least in your own mind) to teen heartthrob can really do a number on your head. Here's how film star Matthew Broderick

(*Ferris Bueller's Day Off*) described his struggles with fame in the *Los Angeles Times*: "I've learned to tune it out, but I have no idea how it's affected my personality. At first it was exciting, then for a while . . . I was nasty to people, and now I'm blank—I'm polite but I don't connect to anybody."

## How to Cope

By now, you've probably decided that all child stars are lonely, conceited, and totally stressed out. Not true! Most young actors are happy kids who love their work and wouldn't trade their fame and fortune for anything. The key is to keep a level head and not take show business—or yourself—too seriously.

Here are a few tricks of the trade:

### Being Normal Begins at Home

**1.** *It's important to realize that being a good actor isn't the same thing as being a good human being.* "We try to tell him 'you've got this ability, but that's not the most important thing in your life,'" explains Noah Gaines's mother. "It's how you treat people and how nice you are."

**2.** *If you aren't pampered at home, you won't act like a spoiled brat on the set.* "I still have my chores to do," Jonathan Taylor Thomas told *Bop*. "I still have to make my bed, vacuum the pool, and clean the cat litter box."

**3.** *Make time for yourself.* When the pressure to succeed gets too intense, Angela Watson says, "I spend a lot of time in my room, listening to my CDs."

**4.** *Remember, home should be a haven—a place you*

can go when show biz gets too crazy. "This is a play-world out here," actor Cassidy Rae (*Clarissa Explains It All, Models Inc.*) told *People.* "I call home and say, 'I need some reality. Talk to me.'"

### Friends and Foes

**1.** *Make friends with kids who like you for yourself, not for your celebrity.* "It can get frustrating when people only know you as the actor kid," Joseph Gordon-Levitt (*Angels in the Outfield*) told *16.* "The kids that get past that are my friends."

**2.** *If you don't talk constantly about your career, neither will your friends.* "We kind of keep it to ourselves," says Robyn Richards's mother. "We don't make a big deal out of it." If Robyn has to miss school to go to a job, she simply tells her friends, "I have to go to L.A. today."

**3.** *If the kids at school get jealous, go out of your way to show them you're a regular kid.* Here's what Matt Jensen did: "There was a girl at my school who was talking to someone and I overheard. She was mad because she thought I was always the center of attention. So I started paying more attention to her until she got over it. Now we're really good friends."

**4.** *Be the person you want to be, not the person other people expect you to be.* "People assume when you're an actress and you're on TV that you love to party and meet exotic people, and get drunk," *Blossom* star Mayim Bialik told *Quake.* "But I'm basically a recluse. I'm a nerd . . . I've never been to a club. It terrifies me. Mostly, I'm just sitting at home."

### Taking Care of Number One

**1.** *Whenever you get a chance to lay low, go for it.* Celebrities sometimes feel like bugs under a microscope. Robyn Richards's mother recalls, "Last week at Lucky's [supermarket] a woman came up and said, 'You're the little girl on *General Hospital*.' And Robyn denied it."

Robyn isn't snubbing people—she just needs a break from all the attention. "They [the fans] want to talk to me for an hour," she explains.

**2.** *Seek out adult actors who are good role models.* When Paul Sutera was starting out in show business, his manager introduced him to former child star Glenn Scarpelli (*One Day at a Time*). "He had a lot of talks with the kids about how to handle this business, and how to handle themselves," Paul's mother says. "And I think because they had seen him on TV, he was credible to them. They listened."

**3.** *Don't let show business become your entire life.* When actor Sean Astin was in Little League, his agent was instructed not to schedule any auditions or jobs that would interfere with his baseball schedule. Sean's parents, former child actor Patty Duke and actor John Astin, knew that their son needed to be a kid first, and a performer second.

**4.** *Don't drink or do drugs.* "I'm healthy, and I like to train and work out and dance and do all that stuff," Aaron Lohr (*Mighty Ducks II*) told *Bop*. "There's always drugs and alcohol at parties . . . I don't do any of that. When you're taking all these foreign substances into your body, it definitely has an effect on you."

**5.** *Don't lose your sense of humor.* "I hope to always keep going straight and not get big-headed," Austin O'Brien (*My Girl 2*) says in *16*. "If I do, I'll take a pin and pop my head!"

**6.** *Finally, be absolutely certain that acting is what you want to do with your life.* If it ever becomes a burden and a chore, it's time to stop. "You have to love the work itself, and I do—it's my life really," Matthew Broderick told the *Los Angeles Times*. "I can remember the first play I did, when I was fifteen. Nervous as I was on stage, I could feel I belonged there. This isn't to say I'm the best actor in the world, but I do know that I'm an actor."

# CHAPTER 10

![star]

# GROWING UP

**I**magine you've got it all—you're a talented actor, you're famous, you're rich, and you're happy. In short, you've got the world by a string. What could possibly go wrong?

Simply this: you grow up. When you stop looking like a kid and start looking like an adult, life changes. Suddenly, you're competing with established adult actors for jobs. But the public—and

> Fame is a hard drug. Quitting fame was harder than any trouble I had with drugs or alcohol.
>
> —*Former child star Paul Petersen*

the casting directors—still think of you as a kid. How can you convince them to accept you in adult roles?

★　★　★

## *What Ever Became of . . . ?*

A few young actors have made the transition to adult stardom. There's Jodie Foster, Rick Schroder, Patty Duke, Johnny Depp, Susan Dey, Melissa Gilbert, and Leonardo DiCaprio, to name a few. You can probably think of some others.

But many former child stars discover that the world wants them to remain a child forever. Here's what Jon Provost, the boy who played Timmy on the TV show *Lassie,* says: "I just got so sick of being called Timmy. . . . After *Lassie* the only part I wanted to play was a cold-blooded killer. But there were no such offers, so I did *The Computer Wore Tennis Shoes* for Disney in 1970 and then I split."

Matthew Broderick, whose biggest hit was the teen film *Ferris Bueller's Day Off,* has continued to work in adult movies. But he still has a tough time escaping his boyish image. "I think I could play evil characters," he told the *Los Angeles Times,* "but the way this business works is, if you're successful at something, everybody wants you to keep doing it again—you know—'Let's get that Ferris Bueller guy.'"

Some child actors prefer to retire when they reach adulthood rather than fight the system. Christopher Knight played Peter on the original *Brady Bunch.* In the book *Bradymania* he says, "I wasn't sure I wanted to be an actor. All my summers were spent doing *The Brady Bunch.* I wanted a normal life. . . . I was dying to meet friends my own age." Today, Chris is the general manager of a software development company.

Others have succeeded as adult actors—but not without a struggle. When *The Brady Bunch* went off the air, Barry Williams (Greg) felt lost. He entered college but dropped out. When he tried to return to acting, he found that no one wanted to hire a twenty-year-old former child star. He was so frustrated and unhappy that he began drinking and gambling.

But Barry's story has a happy ending. He cleaned up his act and eventually found roles in regional theater, including the touring company of the Broadway hit *City of Angels*. Today he still acts onstage—and does the occasional *Brady Bunch* reunion show.

## A Minor Consideration

Paul Petersen was eleven when he was chosen to play the role of Jeff on the ABC-TV series *The Donna Reed Show*. During the next eight years he became one of the hottest teen heartthrobs in the country. It was fun, but it was hard work, too. "I worked every day of my life," he declares. "Not some days, *every* day. No one counts up the hours you spend doing publicity, traveling, signing autographs, being a symbol to other people—but as anyone who has been famous will tell you, that's part of your work."

When *The Donna Reed Show* ended eight years later, Paul was nineteen years old and eager to make the move to adult stardom. But the world still viewed him as cute little Jeff Stone. "In 1966, I worked sixteen weeks," he says. "In 1967, I worked eight weeks. In 1968, I worked four weeks. In 1969, I didn't work at all."

Paul turned to drugs and alcohol. He didn't stop until Mickey Rooney, a former child star himself, sat him down and told him to get out of Hollywood. Paul took the advice. He moved to Connecticut, went to

Paul Petersen (standing behind chair) as he looked on *The Donna Reed Show.*

college, and earned degrees in English and history. Eventually, he became an author of fiction and nonfiction books.

But Paul couldn't forget his child star days and the troubles they had caused him. So he returned to Hollywood and founded an organization called A Minor Consideration to help today's young actors handle the ups and downs of show business.

A Minor Consideration, Paul says, "deals with everything from heroin to hangnails." The organization works with the Young Performers Committee of the Screen Actors Guild to protect child actors' rights, counsels adult stars who work with kids on how to be good role models, and helps child stars and former child stars whose lives are in trouble.

Paul Petersen has many complaints about the way

young actors are treated today. For example, he feels that *all* the money a child actor earns should be put in a trust fund until he is eighteen or older. He also feels that the parents of child actors should be paid a salary for the time they spend on the set caring for their kid. That way, he explains, they wouldn't be tempted to spend their child's money.

But despite Paul's criticisms of the industry, he insists, "I'm not saying kids shouldn't act, I'm saying they ought to be informed. It *can* be done successfully, with a great set of parents."

Here are a few tips for child actors who want to stay successful *and* sane:

## Home Sweet Home

For starters, don't ask your parents to sell your family home. You can rent or buy a condo in L.A., but return to your hometown whenever you aren't working. Remember, Hollywood is Tinseltown. It's not real life. You need to get away every now and then and spend some time living like a normal kid.

Ron Howard (*The Andy Griffith Show, Happy Days*) was one of the most popular child stars ever. Despite Ron's busy schedule, his parents kept their family home in Connecticut and returned to it whenever they could. Today Ron Howard is a well known director (*Apollo 13, Splash, Parenthood*)—and he still has a home in Connecticut.

Henry Thomas starred in the blockbuster *E.T., The Extra-Terrestrial* when he was only ten years old. But his family kept their home in Texas, and when his career began to falter, Henry returned there to attend community college. Now, with his degree in hand, he's back in Hollywood, where he's landed adult roles in the movies *Legends of the Fall* and *Curse of the Starving Class.*

Fourteen-year-old Rider Strong (*Boy Meets World*) and his brother Shiloh (*The Mommies*) grew up in a California town sixty miles north of San Francisco. When the cameras stop rolling, the boys head for their home turf—and their own private tree house. What better way to leave the pressures of Hollywood far behind!

## Save It for a Rainy Day

You should not be the main breadwinner in your family. That's just too much stress to lay on a kid. Instead, your folks should be earning the money, and your salary should be put in a trust fund until you turn eighteen.

In California, there is a law that ensures your parents will do exactly that. It's called the "Coogan Law" after Jackie Coogan, a famous child star in the 1920s who earned millions. When he grew up, Jackie discovered that his mother and stepfather had gained total control of his money—and there was nothing left for him.

The Coogan Law, and other similar state laws, provide that a court petition may be filed seeking a judge's approval of contracts with child entertainers. The petition may be filed by the employer, parent, or guardian of the child. Before the court will grant approval of the contract, the judge will usually demand that a portion of the child's earnings be held in trust until he or she turns eighteen.

Unfortunately, if you land a job but neither your

employer nor your parents file a court petition, you can't control what your parents do with your money. Still, you *can* talk to them and stay informed. If you think your folks don't know how to handle money, you can even suggest that they hire a business manager.

If worse comes to worst, when you turn eighteen, you can request an accounting of your money and how it was spent. It's even possible to go to court sooner and ask to be declared a legal adult. Drew Barrymore did it, and so did Eddie Furlong.

Of course, that's something you'd want to do only if all communication with your parents had broken down. That won't happen if you talk things out and work together. Communication—and a whole lot of love—is the key.

### School Is Cool

"Acting is the only thing I want to do," claims Robyn Richards. But even if you plan on a lifelong career in show business, it's important to keep up your grades.

"If acting is your dream and you want to do it, I would encourage you to pursue it," talent agent Monika Simmons says. "But I always say, 'Go to college.' You can't be desperate [to succeed as an actor] because you will turn casting directors off. You need to be secure enough to know that if this doesn't work out, you have something else."

*Little Big League* star Luke Edwards is prepared for life after stardom. "I want to go to college," he told *Bop,* "and I want to concentrate on education during that portion of my life. After that, I'm not sure. I would like to see where college takes me and if I find any more interests. I don't want to act for the rest of my life because [acting] is pretty cutthroat, and so I don't know if I want to be associated with it for the rest of my life."

Teen heartthrob Joey Lawrence would like to make the move to adult roles, but he knows it isn't easy. "The scripts I've been sent are all for characters that people would expect me to do—you know, Joey Russo—sitcom stuff," he told *16*. "And I don't really want to do that."

To prepare for his uncertain future, Joey is going to college. "I'm starting USC [University of Southern California] . . . and I'm going to study filmmaking 'cause I want to be a director."

## Learn While You Earn

Even if your acting career dries up, you can still have a career in show business. Wendy Lee was a child model and actress in Chicago, Illinois. Now that she's all grown up, she uses her experience and expertise in her current job as a children's talent agent in Denver, Colorado.

Jonathan Brandis hopes to become a director someday. During his off-hours in Orlando, Florida (where *seaQuest DSV* is filmed), he's been "watching real bad TV shows from the '70s—so I can learn how *not* to direct television," he told *People*. He's also wheeling and dealing, trying to find a way to get behind the camera. "I'm actually trying to get in on some Nickelodeon projects right now," he says.

Brian Austin Green (*Beverly Hills 90210*) is branching out into music. "It's totally my creation," he says in *16* about his new album. "I'm doing everything—writing, playing keyboards and drums, singing, and rapping."

There are plenty of show business jobs available behind the scenes, including sound recorder, camera operator, boom operator (the person who holds the microphone), and gaffer (the person who sets up the lights).

You can learn a lot about show business just by hanging around a movie or TV set. "You learn something new every time," Elijah Wood told the *Los Angeles Times*. "You learn a lot of things about sound and film and the camera and stuff."

When you land an acting or modeling job, take the time to talk to the people on the set. Ask the sound man if you can listen through his headphones. Ask the camera operator if you can look through the lens. Ask the makeup artists to show you how they apply makeup.

Who knows? You might discover a new and exciting career.

## Seize the Day

Acting is a crazy business. You never know where your next job is coming from—or if it's coming at all.

So when you are working, enjoy yourself!

Jonathan Brandis knows how important it is to appreciate the present. "The way I look at it is, I didn't expect any of this," he told *People*. "I didn't think at fourteen I'd be working. After [the miniseries] *It*, I thought that was the last big thing I'd do. So right now I'm saying I'm probably not going to be working as an actor in my early twenties. I might be. I don't know."

Fourteen-year-old Trista Barfield has the right attitude. "I've never considered any of the jobs I've done hard," she says in *Kids on Camera*. "I like it a lot, and it is really easy. For me, it's a good feeling to be told I am good and that I am special."

Twelve-year-old Noah Gaines gets a kick out of every play he does. "I love theater," he says eagerly. "I was John in *Peter Pan*, and I got to fly. It was the funnest thing!"

Sixteen-year-old Phillip Glasser loves his life. "I have no stage fright," he declares. "Even the opening night of *Les Miserables* didn't faze me a bit. Ever since I was little, I just liked to perform."

If that sounds like you, then go for it. And no matter what happens—whether you win an Academy Award or only act in one school play—remember always to have fun!

# GLOSSARY

**AFTRA**—American Federation of Television and Radio Artists, the union which represents performers who work on television, radio, and musical recordings.

**Agent**—A person whose job it is to find you work. If you land a job, the agent negotiates the contract. In exchange, he gets paid a commission, usually 10 percent of your salary.

**Audition**—A tryout, a meeting with people who are thinking about hiring you. The people in charge will tell you what to do. They might give you some lines to read, ask you to improvise, or just chat with you. This is your chance to show your stuff.

**Blocking**—An actor's specific movements and positioning onstage. If the performance is being filmed, the director will decide where the cameras will be positioned during each scene and how the actors will move around the set.

**Breakdowns**—Casting notices circulated to agents and managers daily by Breakdown Services of West Hollywood.

**Call sheet**—A schedule of scenes to be shot each day, the length of each scene, the location, who will be in the shots, and what time the actors must report for work.

**Callback**—An additional audition after your first audition for a part. This follow-up audition means you're still being considered for the part.

**Casting director**—A person who finds, auditions, and hires actors. The casting director is hired by the producer of the project, given the script, and told to find actors to play the parts.

**Cattle call**—An open audition to which hundreds of people come to try out for a role. You don't have to have an agent or belong to a union to go to a cattle call.

**Cold reading**—Reading your lines on the spot, without any practice.

**Composite**—A professional photograph of you that shows you in two or three poses, wearing different clothes and hairstyles.

**Crew**—The nonactors who work on TV shows, movies, and plays behind the scenes. The crew includes technicians, costume designers, makeup people, tutors, electricians, and so on.

**Cut**—The word used by the director to alert everyone that he wants to stop filming, either because the scene is over or because he wants to correct a mistake.

**Headshot**—A professional photograph of you, usually 8" by 10", which you give out at auditions. Headshots may also be mailed to agents and managers.

**Industrial**—A short movie, made by a company, that promotes the company's product or teaches their employees about their jobs. Industrials are not shown to the public. They are shown within the company or at trade shows and conventions.

**Location**—A place where a film or photographs are shot, other than a TV or movie studio. If a film is shot "on location" in a city, the actors and crew are filming on the streets or in and around actual city buildings.

**Manager**—A person whose job it is to guide your career. He introduces you to important people, helps you decide which jobs to take, and manages your business dealings. He cannot actually send you out on auditions (only an agent is licensed to do that), but he can work with your agent to decide which auditions you should go to. In return, he is paid a commission, usually 20 percent of your salary.

**Monologue**—A solo speech, often used by an actor to audition for a play.

**Residuals**—Additional payments received by a performer when commercials, TV shows, or print ads are rebroadcast or reprinted after the initial broadcast or publication.

**Resume**—A one-page listing of your credits: all the performances you've done, any training you've had, and any special talents you possess.

**SAG**—Screen Actors Guild, the union that represents performers who work on film.

**Sides**—A copy of the script containing only the lines you will be required to speak.

**Sign-in sheet**—A piece of paper at an audition, on which you write your name, the name of your agent, the time you arrived, and the time you leave.

**Wrap**—The word used to indicate that a scene or project is finished to everyone's satisfaction. The director will announce, "That's a wrap!"

# RECOMMENDED READING

Callan, K. *The Los Angeles Agent Book*. Studio City, Calif.: Sweden Press, 1994.

Cassidy, David, with Deffaa, Chip. *C'Mon, Get Happy*. New York: Warner Books, 1994.

Friedman, Ginger Howard. *Callback*. New York: Bantam, 1993.

Kramer, Susan, and Walker, Kim Robert. *So You Want To Get Your Child into Commercials*. W/K Associates, 1993.

Padol, Brian A., and Simon, Alan. *The Young Performer's Guide*. Crozet, Va.: Betterway Publications, 1990.

Stancil, Eva, and Steiner, Cynthia. *Kids on Camera*. Atlanta: Peachtree Publications, 1990.

Steele, William Paul. *Stay Home and Star!* Portsmouth, N.H.: Heinemann Educational Books, 1992.

# BIBLIOGRAPHY

"Aaron Parties Smart," *Bop,* September 1994.

"Big Screen Boys Tell All," *16,* November 1994.

"Blossom!" *Quake,* Summer 1995.

Brady, James, "In Step with: Hilary Swank," *Parade Magazine,* August 7, 1994.

Callan, K. *The Los Angeles Agent Book.* Studio City, Calif.: Sweden Press, 1994.

"Campin' Out with Jonathan Jackson," *16,* November 1994.

Cassidy, David, with Deffaa, Chip. *C'Mon, Get Happy* New York: Warner Books, 1994.

"Crazy 4 Chris!" *16,* July 1994.

"The Days & Nights of Rider Strong," *Bop,* December 1994.

"Duck Talk," *16,* July 1994.

Dutka, Elaine, "Unmasking Eric Stoltz," *Los Angeles Times,* September 4, 1994.

"Elijah is Set to Learn," *Bop,* December 1994.

"Everybody's Lovin' Elijah," *16,* September 1994.

Friedman, Ginger Howard. *Callback*. New York: Bantam, 1993.

"Get the Stats on Luke Edwards," *16,* September 1994.

Gliatto, Tom, "Catch of the Day," *People Weekly,* August 29, 1994.

Goodman, Mark, "Winsome Twosome," *People Weekly,* May 9, 1994.

Green, Joey. *The Partridge Family Album*. New York: Harper Perennial, 1994.

Halliwell, Leslie. *Halliwell's Filmgoer's and Video Viewer's Companion*. 9th ed. New York: Harper & Row, 1988.

Honeycutt, Kirk, "Fourteen-year-old Boy in 3-Film Deal at Paramount," *The Hollywood Reporter,* August 9, 1994.

"Hot From Hollywood," *Bop,* September 1994.

"Hot From Hollywood," *Bop,* December 1994.

"Jason, Austin, Elijah," *16,* July 1994.

"Joey & Matt—This 'N That," *16,* November 1994.

"Jon: Come Inside My Dressing Room," *16,* November 1994.

"Joseph Gordon-Levitt," *16,* October 1994.

"Just a Regular Joe," *Bop,* December 1994.

"Kickin' It with Hilary Swank," *16,* October 1994.

Kramer, Susan, and Walker, Kim Robert. *So You Want To Get Your Child into Commercials.* W/K Associates, 1993.

Lamparski, Richard. *Whatever Became of . . . ?* New York: Crown, 1989.

Lipton, Michael A., "Model of Virtue," *People Weekly,* July 18, 1994.

McKenna, Kristine, "A Little Song, A Little Dance," *Los Angeles Times,* October 30, 1994.

McKenna, Kristine, "Mary Steenburgen," *Los Angeles Times,* September 18, 1994.

McNeil, Alex. *Total Television.* New York: Penguin Books, 1991.

"Meet the So-Called Buds From *My So-Called Life,*" *16,* November 1994.

*Modeling, Commercials & Acting.* Beverly Hills, Calif: O'Brien Productions, 1992. (video)

Moran, Elizabeth. *Bradymania.* Holbrook, Mass.: Bob Adams, Inc., 1992.

O'Brien, Betsy. *Luke Perry*. New York: Modern Publishing, 1991.

Padol, Brian A., and Simon, Alan. *The Young Performer's Guide*. Crozet, Va: Betterway Publications, 1990.

Pearlman, Cindy, "Newest Brat Pack Not Really So Bratty," *Santa Barbara News-Press,* August 15, 1994.

Schindehette, Susan, "Feline Groovy," *People Weekly,* August 1, 1994.

Schindehette, Susan, "Life after *Life Goes On,*" *People Weekly,* May 2, 1994.

"A Sign of Jonathan Jackson's Status," *Bop,* December 1994.

"16 Summer Movie Blow-out!" *16,* October 1994.

"16 Things You Didn't Know About Rider Strong," *16,* November 1994.

Stancil, Eva, and Cynthia Steiner. *Kids on Camera* Atlanta: Peachtree Publications, 1990.

"The Stats on Luke Edwards," *Bop,* September 1994.

Steele, William Paul. *Stay Home and Star!* Portsmouth, N.H.: Heinemann Educational Books, 1992.

Tagami, Ty. "Sean Nelson, the Sundance Kid," *Los Angeles Times,* September 4, 1994.

"Teen Stars Steam Up the Summer Soaps," *16,* October 1994.

"These New Kids Keep Up With An Oscar Winner," *Parade Magazine,* December 12, 1993.

Vanore, Fred. *A Parents' Guide to Successful Child Modeling,* Wayne, N.J.: Vanore Productions, 1992.

Wallace, Nora K., "For Teens at PCPA Event, the Play Is Really the Thing," *Santa Barbara News-Press,* August 29, 1994.

Weinraub, Bernard, "For Young Actor, Art Imitates Life," *Santa Barbara News-Press,* July 22, 1994.

Zierold, Norman J. *The Child Stars.* New York: Coward-McCann, 1965.